ART HOPE

The Way To Creative Wellness

Laura Jaquays

ART HOPE PRESS

Ogunquit, Maine USA

ART HOPE PRESS
Ogunquit, Maine 03907 - USA
arthope.org
laurajaquays.com

Cover artwork "Creative Being" by Laura Jaquays
Cover design by Kristy Cavaretta
Author portrait by Khristine Kostis

ART HOPE The Way To Creative Wellness
by Laura Jaquays

Printed in USA
Library of Congress Control Number: 2020915292

ISBN 978-0-9975078-2-9

Contents

Preface

Like the flow of creativity, the genesis of *ART HOPE* becoming this book was organic, written in ripples and floods of inspiration and perspiration. The first version took seven years to organize and express my ideas in the words on these pages. I've updated and enriched the content because creativity is a work in progress and I'm learning more every day about the benefits to health and well-being.

I am an artist, arts educator, and founder of ART HOPE, a nonprofit dedicated to creative wellness education. With art in my heart and hope in my soul, I am a seeker and wayshower of creative wellness in my practice and in the community arts programs I teach. It is my life's work and greatest joy to give everyday creativity a language that helps people recognize how they are creative and ways to cultivate a healthful, artful life.

Many things *moved* me to write this book. What compelled me most is when I'm teaching expressive arts, people of all ages often say, "I am not creative." Words no creature should ever speak! Many people have feelings of anxiety about not being good at "art". Art is all the products of human creativity. We are all creative beings. The book is about us. It's for the many, not the few. The animated theories presented are a manifesto for creative wellness and a positive philosophy for living that will inspire a new mantra, "I am creative." *ART HOPE* is an opus to creativity for everyone, everywhere, every day.

From theory to practice, my artist-who-loves-science interpretation of creativity explores the wellness benefits of art-making, art-taking, and art-giving. Are creative people happier and healthier? Empirical science has yet to adequately measure the quantitative impacts to the human condition. Neuroscientists, doctors, psychologists, philosophers, cultural commentators, and curious writers are currently reporting the physical, emotional, and social benefits of creativity. By its very nature, creativity is qualitative and more complex than statistics and theories can define. Most importantly, people tend to feel good when they are doing creativity. The positive energy of feeling good when doing a loved creative activity affects health and well-being in beneficial ways.

There is no single method that explains or teaches creativity. This is a good thing. It involves the mind-body-spirit and all the senses. Like happiness, love, and faith, the qualitative benefits are a positive growth mindset, improved well-being, and it brings meaning to life. Creativity transforms something common into an uncommon thing that is new and better. It defies descriptions and data.

My writing is based on widely published information and informed by stories, metaphors, anecdotes, cultural references, art history, ancient wisdom, practical models, common sense, and personal belief. Together, the work reflects my lifetime of research and self-directed learning, and my artistic observations as a student of natural things. I offer the book as a reference for seekers with the hope it begins a larger community conversation about creative wellness.

An open book is like an open heart. *ART HOPE* reflects my creative process and is a "work" of art and how I express myself as a community artist. My work in the studio (painting and writing) and experience in the field (teaching creative wellness) are all interconnected and growing. As this project evolves, the goal for www.arthope.org is to build our online creative wellness resources. Books and curriculum products are published by ART HOPE PRESS. To support this much-loved work, my author's proceeds are donated to the nonprofit organization for the expansion of online creative wellness education.

I encourage readers to *move* through the book at your own pace and to explore your creativity. Learn ways to engage in creative self-expression and self-care. Use *ART HOPE* as a practical guide and a way to *motivate* your purpose and passion. Take the ideas off the page and apply what you know and love to be the artist-in-residence in your life. Enjoy. CREATE!

Laura Jaquays
Ogunquit, Maine

Gratitude

We are all angels here to help each other. *ART HOPE* was written on a wing and a prayer and with inspiration and encouragement from the special people in my life who have recognized and nurtured my creativity. They are my teachers, mentors, friends, and family, and all the kind souls who have participated in my programs and shared wonderful conversations about creativity and life. Thanks for your love and support.

I am grateful for the experience of writing this volume, for the joy of self-expression and countless hours of self-discipline and hard work, and those few dark moments of self-doubt that strengthened my self-confidence and *motivation* to tell this story. If you've ever wanted to write a book or pursue a creative idea or dream, do it. Don't wait. Be curious, fearless, and open. Be present and practice your creativity. Be your purpose and passion. On the path to expressing creative true voice you will meet the co-creators who will inspire you to be your best self. Recognize your angels, with love and gratitude.

Introduction

ART HOPE is a practical guide for healthful, artful living that explores the healing opportunities of art-making, art-taking, and art-giving. Creativity is a ready remedy for everyone, everywhere, every day that reduces stress and increases wellness. It is an essential life skill and our most renewable and valuable natural resource. This positive growth mindset helps us survive and thrive.

Creativity is a *movement*, a generative and regenerative energy that maintains a state of balance and homeostasis. It articulates life. Throughout the book, words related to the fluidity and flow of this *motion* are italicized to emphasize the importance of the corporeal nature of creative activity. To gain the benefits requires the body to be in the present moment, in mind and spirit, and to practice creativity. Creative thinking, doing, and being activates wellness. The instinct to express our ideas and emotions naturally *motivates* the process with a rhythmic energy that animates purpose and illuminates passion. It transforms and *moves* us to make an order from the chaos of living, to invent something beautiful and practical, and to understand and express the meaning of life. This primal *movement* is linked to creating health. Like creative energy, health is not stagnant. We can create health and a good life.

Wellness is a dynamic, hopeful state of positive health in mind, body, and spirit, in any moment or environment, that nurtures the creative potential in all aspects of living. It exalts our best qualities and is an empowered state that takes time to develop. The things that make us well are relative to our life condition. Wellness is a healthy personal balance. Creative wellness is the measure of our health, happiness, and creativity in everyday experience. Research shows when people have a creative and positive approach to life, it activates the "hope factor" and the body's natural ability to self-heal, triggering a placebo effect.

Creative therapies in various forms are widely recommended by healthcare providers for patient well care because the process reduces stress. A leading cause of illness, stress negatively impacts our health, work, relationships, and daily life. It can be minimized with a preventive daily dose of Vitamin C-reativity. At every age, creativity enriches learning and memory, supports emotional and physical health, promotes mindfulness and happiness, and celebrates life. *ART HOPE* is a cradle to grave perspective for people seeking to improve their health and well-being through creative self-expression and self-care.

How are you creative? The common things people do and love to do are creative. We are creative creatures. It is a human capacity and phenomenon we all share and how our species evolves with a sense of wonder and empathy for life. It is the natural way we relate to ourselves, others, and the world around us. Our responsive creative nature is activated in any environment through the senses. This is the conscious and un-conscious experience of what we think and feel involving our sight, sound, touch, smell, and taste. Our intuitive sense in-volves all perception and is the portal of inspiration.

The things that inspire us and the ways we practice cre-ativity are unique and personal. We each have a creative true voice that needs and desires to be expressed. *ART HOPE* will help you discover, develop, and express yours. It says, "I am creative". It is the realm of peak creative experience. The native confidence to create is a positive force waiting for you to know it, claim it, nurture it, love it, and be it in the world. It doesn't re-quire any special skills or technical equipment, just you being creative, self-actualized and self-expressed. Creativity is the way to wellness.

What is everyday creativity? To facilitate the big picture and a bigger conversation, I offer the *ART HOPE Creative Wellness Model*. It is a universal application for everyday creativity that relates to our lifestyles, interests, workplace, education, healthcare, corporations, and communities and leadership, locally and globally. Together, the model and essays represent the many ways people are creative. They highlight mental, physical, spiritual, environment, community, home, language, sound, and visual aspects. These nine themes are interconnected and suggest the organic potential of creativity. Most of us can relate to some interest or activity described in the model. Use the concept as an idea catcher to spark creativity, prompt an interest or hobby, and help identify opportunities for your expression.

The nine aspects illustrate a basic model for creative living. **MENTAL**, **PHYSICAL**, and **SPIRITUAL** relate to the mind-body-spirit connection. This is our creative thinking, doing, and being - the experiential trinity inherent in all creative processes. **ENVIRONMENT, COMMUNITY**, and **HOME** relate to belonging and a sense of place. **LANGUAGE**, **SOUND**, and **VISUAL** relate to the expression of thoughts and feelings. **Love** is the universal energy that inspires and *motivates* creativity. We need all these aspects in a healthy balance.

Doing creativity requires giving yourself the time, space, and tools needed for your expression. Especially, time, *me-time* in real-time for the mindfulness of creative practice. Having the time to create balance in our lives is the key to wellness. It is a challenge for most people. Often, there are too many distractions and responsibilities that steal our attention and drain energy. Like any healthful habit, the discipline to make personal time to be present and prepared to create is basic.

A creative practice doesn't happen in isolation. As singularly as it manifests, the individual needs a communal relationship. The process is solo or shared, and it's always a collaboration, a synthesis of everyone and everything that makes it happen. We are co-creators who work in a synergistic relationship with our thoughts, feelings, ideas, habits, materials, books, methods, themes, environments, challenges, opportunities, schedules, peers, and instructors. Co-creators are what and who supports creativity.

ART HOPE is the way to creative wellness. Recognize and practice your creativity. *Motivate* your purpose and passion. You can do it!

Part One: Healthful, Artful Life

1: Creative Creatures

It's the nature of life to create and re-create. The human impulse to innovate and improve is how we survive and thrive in our environment. Life requires creative skills. With original thought and expression, we make an order from chaos, the formless into a form. This innate ability inspires us to make art and tools, both beautiful and practical, and gives purpose and meaning to life. Art is all the products of human creativity, every form of expression and perception. It teaches us about humanity and history. **Art**ifacts of earlier creatures and cultures are evidence of our existence and lived experience. Past, present, and future, individually and collectively, creativity is the way we communicate ideas and emotions, cultivate talents and interests, and use our knowledge and empathy to make the world better.

Creativity transforms something common into an original and uncommon thing that is valued and enjoyed. From ancient engineers of the wheel to modern inventors of the computer, creativity is a basic human quality. We are makers and builders, dreamers and achievers, creators who manufacture the basics required for daily living. It includes our food, shelter, methods of survival and sustenance, and all forms of communication and mobility. In balance, we use creativity to express ourselves in ways that speak to the spirit, show our love and compassion, and celebrate life.

We are artisans of life. We originate and create. Expressivity, the quality of conveying thoughts and feelings, is intrinsic to the human creative experience. We express and **art**iculate our aliveness in sensory and emotional ways. The art of healing touch and song soothes a child. The art of weaving crafts a basket to hold the garden's colorful harvest. The art of cooking inspires seasoning that special sauce for those we love. The art of tinkering and problem solving improves our life condition. The genius of telling a good joke enhances the art of friendship we share with others. Everyday creativity is all the things we naturally do and love to do, and how we express our uniquely human nature at its best.

Our creative being loves being creative. Creativity is an instinctive process that *moves* us to generate and regenerate our energy and resources. The rhythms of nature prompt inborn timing and active functioning in response to our environment and the need to self-sustain. Creativity is a natural force that activates the cycles of all life. This energy animates expression and fuels thriving, which stimulates the primal *movement* linked to creating good mind-body-spirit health. It plugs in the body electric and illuminates our native confidence to create. It is human instinct to make our mark or match - to create an original expression of what we internally think and feel, or to interpret what we observe in external experience. It is an organic proclivity that comes from the soul and helps us know and relate what is knowable and relatable.

Creativity is a positive growth mindset. It is common sense, a proactive life-enhancing process that *motivates* us to create opportunities from obstacles, happiness from sadness, abundance from the seeds of our thoughts and feelings. We are inspired to create what we see and don't see, what we need and desire. Creativity makes us observers of all things in nature and our human nature. We are intelligent, imaginative, and curious, and because we wonder and endeavor to ask unanswerable questions, civilization advances. We are empathic, compassionate, and hopeful, and because we love and aspire to make a better life for ourselves and others, humanity evolves.

Nature is the model for life and art. Cycles of creation and re-creation transfer the energy that makes life possible. The natural *movement* of creativity is like a pebble tossed into still water, causing the ripples to flow and *move* rhythmically in an exchange of energy that affects the larger whole. Gravitational waves ripple in time and space. When they collide in a big BANG! a crystalline change happens. Like resonates like to create a new form. Two become one, the one becomes the infinite as creator and co-creator merge, *move*, and change. Creative energy orders or reorders itself in random and designed ways, transforming one state into another. In *motion*, energy cannot be destroyed, only transformed.

Creativity is a self-nurturing, self-*motivating* process. Once sensed, we naturally seek more of this positive homeostasis. *Moving* and transforming energy is essential to healing. Human nature responds to nurture. It activates the creative cycles of growth and change that produce more creativity, more growth, and more change. Like mirrors like and *moves* the energy to restore balance from an unbalanced state. The organic laws of nature and creativity follow the alchemy of how one thing transforms another with an enlivened energy, causing an effect. It is the creative source. A spark of life that transforms energy from one state to another, from an old order to a brilliant new form of chaos, that perpetuates the remarkable human capacity to create.

This organic symmetry is energetically part of an asymmetrical process, and vice versa, that reflects the essential *movement* of the Universe. There is a balance of parallel energies, positive and negative, known and unknown, that stretch and compress to construct our life existence and experience. The quantitative ways creative energy changes are the realm of science, which seeks to define in theory what is practical and knowable. The qualitative ways creative energy changes are the realm of art, which seeks to understand the beauty and mystery of life and to express its essence. Creativity is activated by the primal *movement* of this cause and effect, a force that is never stagnant in an ever-changing landscape of time and space. It is *motivated* by our needs, desires, and a powerful human will for creative self-actualization and self-expression.

In metaphor, the pebble is the asymmetrical force of matter *moving* through space as it is controlled by gravity. Then, with a *splash!* of change, the still water *moves!* causing a wave to spiral and flow in a transformed state. As the pebble hits the water, it activates a new energetic force. Creativity is in *motion.* The pebble is a co-creator that excites change. It is a big idea, a creative thing we love to do, a teacher, a tool, a fundamental requirement, a light in the darkness, the seed of everything, our inspired will. The creative source is the cause and effect in *motion.* The waves and particles of our activated creative energy may hit some random chaos and destruction as they ebb and flow, because creativity is like that - a little release, a little resistance, or a lot of both - and a lot can happen to a pebble along the way as it flows with the ever-changing currents of life in real-time and space.

Like all good creation metaphors, the pebble chaotically destroys the water's balance and its perceived order, while creating a new balance and form of energy that engenders change. Up, down, and all around, our inborn creativity *moves* with the energetic cycles of nature and the Universe. As it is above, so below. There is no standard model that explains the miraculous energizing spark that sets our human creative thinking, doing, and being in *motion,* which is why it remains such a fascinating field of scientific study. In a unified theory, the world's most imaginative scientists may discover that the dynamic energy of human creativity, the expansion and contraction, the cause and effect, the glorious chaos that makes a new order, the purpose and passion - is the same stuff that makes up our great Universe and all that is beyond.

The anthropological story of creativity is a cross-pollination of art and science that has inspired some of the world's greatest intellectual and artistic individuals. Science and art are creative ways to understand chaos and order, to discover and invent, to ask and answer, and to observe the nature of things as they relate to our human condition and the cosmos. Both are mysterious, awe-inspiring states of flow that are mutually sympathetic in their asymmetry. Artists intuitively know how to express the physics of color and light. Scientists technically know how to explain it. When asked, most theoretical physicists will tell you their favorite tool is the imagination. Creativity drives change and brilliant breakthroughs in art and science and all aspects of life. And so, our story begins with a universal symbol for creativity in *motion* from history's most extraordinary artist-scientist.

Leonardo da Vinci (1452-1519) was a brilliant Italian artist, architect, engineer, mathematician, and natural scientist. He was a visionary polymath and inventor who was mostly self-taught. The genius of his legendary notebooks illustrates that he was a dedicated observer and knower of nature and how things work. In his time, Leonardo embodied the Renaissance concept that every human being possesses an innate and limitless capacity to develop knowledge and expression. In his iconic drawing, *Vitruvian Man,* he solves the metaphorical design of a circle that is squared to align with a human form at the center of the Universe, the creative point of origin by which all is measured and perceived. It was an important focus for architects, mathematicians, and scientists in the fifteenth century to prove this geometric connection was a humanistic symbol for how "man" was a microcosm of the macrocosm. In your mind's eye, you know the drawing. It's that naked guy doing jumping jacks, also known as *Cosmic Man*. For a visual reference I've drawn the modern illustration on the book's cover based on Leonardo's famous work, which I've named *Creative Being*. It is an archetype for creativity in *motion*. I am more of an artist than a scientist. My rendering represents the animated and **art**iculated *movement* of creativity as an elemental life force. I apply this visual theory to how people are creative, as individuals and communities. I propose, when in *motion*, this natural energy activates our positive potential to create wellness and a healthy balance.

Look at the cover illustration and visualize the dynamics in the classic diagram. A singular androgynous figure symbolically stands at the center of the cosmos in an axis that represents its alignment with humankind. The form has a medial foothold in both worlds - conscious and unconscious, earthly and heavenly, physical and metaphysical. The circle represents Heaven with the body expanding out towards the cosmos. The square is Earth with the body standing in balance on a physical plane. The arms and legs are extended, like the spokes of a wheel in *motion*, and superimposed in two positions to illustrate the human form in geometric proportion. The figure stands symmetrically inside the circle, inscribed by the square, which is asymmetrically centered and adjusted to fit the architecture of the human body and center of mass. This is how Leonardo's historic work visually solves the ancient geometric problem of squaring a circle, by representing that the human individual is the center axis of both. The body is standing balanced on the physical plane, while reaching out to their higher creative nature and a higher power. Conjoined, we can see that the relationship of the limbs animates the figure. Expanding and contracting, stretching and compressing, this *movement* is symbolic of the life force energy and flow of creativity.

The design exalts the human form which is seemingly in *motion* and in-sync in mind-body-spirit. It is fully illuminated, immersed in all the colors of expression with love emanating from the heart, a centering focus. It models how the asymmetric *movement* of creativity animates our interconnectedness to all things to achieve equipoise. This relates to the sovereign creative power of the individual, self-actualized and self-expressed, balanced and empowered, present and standing in one's self. *Creative Being* **art**iculates the liberating *movement* of being creative with purpose and passion.

Our purpose is to live a meaningful life. It is not one thing or a big accomplishment that defines us. Purpose is the engine of our work in progress lives and can evolve and change as we do. It is our calling, when we are doing what we do best in ways that make us feel appreciated and life better. It is selfhood, an alignment of work, relationships, and beliefs that gives agency and engenders a healthy self-ownership and self-confidence. Change *motivates* purpose and offers a new perspective. It is self-knowledge and knowing what we are born to do, when we hear the call to action of our creative true voice. More importantly, purpose is about our creative presence, not productivity. Purpose is a *motivator* intrinsic to creativity and essential to human evolution.

Passion is an immersion in the people and things we love. If we have a strong purpose, it is passionately kindled by our enthusiasm and emotional intensity. It is why we do what we love because we want and need to do it, for ourselves and others. Passion fuels work, relationships, and beliefs, and is the spark of life. It's the eternal flame that keeps the faith and warms the heart, and no matter how far we roam it feels like home. Our passion is what makes creativity a peak experience and why it feels so good. Passion *moves* us with the weightless gravity of love. It fuels the desire to make a change and transform our creative thinking, doing, and being. Love inspires, and loving and being loved builds a foundation of strength for being our creative purpose and passion.

With love at your center, imagine yourself in the same position as our symbol, *Creative Being*, who will teach us more in this story of creative wellness. Now, think about your creativity *moving* and visualize yourself doing it. YOU, animated and **art**iculated, empowered by being and becoming your best creative self. Throughout this book, words related to the fluidity and flow of this *motion* are italicized to prompt you to *lean* into your creativity and *move* your energy toward healthful, artful living. Creativity is an essential life skill and our most renewable and valuable natural resource. It is a basic human quality that helps us survive and thrive. We create what makes us whole and well. Creative thinking illuminates the mind, creative doing articulates the body, and creative being expresses the spirit.

2: The Other Vitamin C

Creativity in *motion* is an agent of change which causes an effect that either calms or rouses. This dynamic energy naturally restores vitality. People respond to creative experiences differently. Something rousing for you may be calming for me, and something calming for you may be rousing for me. The energy goes to the need, the remedy finds the wound. A creative process activates thinking, doing, and being. It relaxes or stimulates relative to capacities and interests and functions with a *motivational* intensity that creates a healthy balance. Creativity is the other Vitamin C. Similar to the common essential nutrient L-ascorbic acid, a daily dose of Vitamin C-reativity helps build the immune system. A scientific cure is not the only route to health. Wellness is created with a positive attitude and engaging in an active creative lifestyle.

Developing creative self-care strategies to manage negative factors and minimize stress in our lives is preventive when part of a proactive wellness routine. The big "C" helps maintain good health because it reduces stress, a leading cause of illness and disease. Stress is the burden of emotional and physical demands on the human body. We respond to it relative to our life condition. Our physical state, as well as psychological issues and personal circumstances, affects health for better or worse.

Stress kills healthy cells and depresses the immune system. It also raises the risk of heart disease and high blood pressure, contributes to depression and anxiety, interferes with sleep, impairs thinking, negatively impacts weight and nutrition, and is a significant factor in aging. Chronic stress which accumulates during a lifetime of negative conditioning, overwork, or trauma, batters the immune responses and destroys adrenal function. It releases cortisol, a life-sustaining hormone that is essential to maintaining homeostasis. Cortisol regulates the body's capacity to respond to stress and is toxic at high levels. Too much of the "fight or flight" response damages organs and suppresses the autonomic nervous system. Maintaining a creative self-care practice is an excellent way to restore the balance needed to manage the stresses of modern life. We are sicker when we are not happy and not creative. Less stress = more health. More creativity = less illness.

From illness to wellness, doing a creative activity is an effective method for stress reduction. Whether we are art-making, *the experience of creating*, art-taking, *experiencing what is created*, or art-giving, *sharing a creative experience,* the process engages the present moment by focusing our attention beyond stress and towards positive living. It happens when we practice our favorite creative things. Like taking a walk in the park, spending time with a friend, solving a crossword puzzle, listening to birds sing, working in the garden, tinkering with a home project, cooking for a party, doodling and dreaming, or having a good laugh. Biological, physiological, and neurological studies of everyday creativity represent an emerging field of research with a compelling body of evidence that shows its positive effects on the human condition. Without the need for a doctor's prescription, you can enjoy the wellness benefits.

BENEFITS OF EVERYDAY CREATIVITY
- reduces stress
- promotes relaxation or stimulation
- boosts the immune system
- supports good mental health
- facilitates self-expression and self-care

- prompts wonder, curiosity, and play
- creates community connections
- nurtures mindfulness and awakens the senses
- inspires and celebrates life

Wellness is a dynamic, hopeful state of positive health in mind, body, and spirit, in any moment or environment, that nurtures the creative potential in all aspects of living. It exalts our best qualities and is an empowered state that takes time to develop. The things that make us well are relative to our life condition. Wellness is a healthy personal balance, a mind-body-spirit alignment. Creative wellness is the measure of our health, happiness, and creativity in daily life experience. It's the realm of peak creative experience and our creative true voice.

Wellness is not a product. It is a way of living that makes us feel well and whole. It is not an elitist state. Wellness is for everyone. We all need it to survive and thrive. It's the healthy self-optimization and self-awareness that is essential to human flourishing. Wellness isn't always a perfect state. It can be a delicate and often difficult balance with life's realities, an ongoing negotiation of time, work, and responsibilities while taking care of basic needs. Wellness is our health-wealth and happiness. For most people, having physical and emotional well-being is more important than money. Wellness is what we value most and how we live well.

Making the time for creative self-expression and self-care is essential to maintaining personal balance. Self-care is not an indulgence. A lack of attention to basic needs is the quickest way to burn out. It can be hard to catch-up and repair the damage to health and relationships. Taking *me-time* is the key to wellness. If we don't take the time to care for ourselves, we can't care for others and be our best.

Can we create health? The mind and body are one. All physiology is linked to the brain which brilliantly powers the nervous system to run bodily functions. Homeostasis is the wisdom of the body that allows us to maintain a stable, constant condition while internal and external environments are changing. The theory was popularized in the book, *The Wisdom Of The Body* by Walter B. Cannon (1897-1947), a Harvard physiology professor who described the synergistic relationship of mental and physical functions, and first used the term "fight or flight response".

Optimal health is a result of a mind-body balance. For a healing protocol to adequately care for the physical body it must integrate psychological, emotional, and environmental factors and everything else that is impacting one's life condition. Healing is a multidimensional process. If we approach it in a linear way, the wisdom of the body is not revealed and our natural healing powers remain untapped.

Psychoneuroimmunology links the interaction of the brain, endocrine, and immune systems in relation to psychological processes and health. This natural form of intuitive medicine is the body's way of preventing disease. The human mind-body is incredibly efficient in the business of health. The body reflects the way we think, act, and feel. Through psycho-neuro-immunology we are able to condition the immune system to prevent illness. When we engage the mighty powers of the mind to create health, the body can thrive. Peak mind = peak body.

Experiential creativity activates the health-enhancing mind-body connection. It stabilizes heart rate and increases oxygen saturation levels in the blood. It engages the brain in ways that release endorphins, a class of hormones located in the hypothalamus and pituitary gland. These endorphins, also known as endogenous morphine, function as neurotransmitters and when activated resemble an opiate with the capacity to produce analgesia and feelings of well-being. The effects reduce stress and balance other factors related to illness, such as pain and inflammation. Dopamine is another feel-good neurotransmitter released through creativity that is associated with learning, pleasure, and reward-seeking behavior. The biology of creativity works symbiotically to relieve stress and mitigate pain by promoting relaxation or stimulation, and drawing our energy and attention towards an expressive experience. Consciously and unconsciously, the creative mind guides the body to healing.

A creative process activates the inner physician. Natural therapeutic effects come from the experience and sensory memory of the experience of art-making, art-taking, and art-giving. Generally, we are creatively *motivated* by what inspires us. We tend to feel good when we are doing a loved creative thing. The positive energy of feeling good when doing a loved creative thing affects health.

The cause and effect of creative energy in *motion* functions as an agent of change that transforms one state into another. This positive influence impacts health and well-being. It happens when we are physically still in meditation or actively doing a creative task. The flow of this energy enlivens sensory awareness. What we see, hear, touch, smell, and taste informs how we articulate life. It is generative and regenerative energy that *moves* in and through us, the osmosis of *motivation* and creation that conveys expression and impels action.

The multidimensional nature of creativity heightens sensory perception and transmits vibrations that flow through meridians in the body. This life-giving force of universal energy, known in ancient Chinese culture as chi, is our essential vitalism. It's the energy that keeps us alive at a cellular and spiritual level. It calms or rouses, relaxes or excites, or both; creating an equilibrium of stimuli and healing energy that naturally finds its way to the need. Healing happens when we are in the moment, expressing creative true voice with the right balance and relationship to ourselves and others. Regardless of one's state of physical health, and even with dis-ease, creativity promotes positive psychology and enriches well-being.

Our mind and body cannot be strong without the spirit. It is the natural center of our being where the inspired will to be well dwells. It fuels the desire to create life with every breath and heartbeat. The spirit rhythmically sparks inspiration and enlivens positive energy. With the mind-body-spirit in healing harmony, we can enlist the "hope factor" by doing creativity. Scientific research shows when people have a positive and creative approach to life, it activates the hope factor and the body's natural ability to self-heal, triggering a measurable placebo effect.

Hope is inner-medicine, a built-in immunological response. It's a belief in the power to heal that comes from our capacity to create good health and a good life. This psychological optimism overcomes negative thoughts, reduces stress and anxiety, and engenders the resilience and strength that is needed to cope with our challenges and disadvantages. Hope opens a window to the future and the fresh flow that rejuvenates. The resolve to create health stimulates the body's immune system and a healing state of equipoise through our positive intention and belief. It is the magic of cause and effect. Wellness is a will to be well.

Medical studies refer to the placebo effect when an innocuous medication has resulted in beneficial biochemical changes due to the person's faith in the treatment. The placebo effect has long been part of traditional and nontraditional medicine. This phenomenon, and the promise of health, is the science behind drug trials when a patient participant is treated with either a placebo or the real drug. The word "placebo" is the Latin verb for *I shall please.* It is designed to unlock the body's natural medicine cabinet. A placebo drug can be potent, even though science isn't quite sure how it works. Our environment and attitude impacts the placebo effect. Positive thoughts and actions create positive thoughts and actions. Energy follows intention. Disharmony is akin to disease in a reciprocal and sympathetic relationship. As we believe, so we will be. Creative healing energy makes more creative healing energy. We respond to nurture and positive belief. The human body is made of trillions of cells, and the dynamic of all that energy *moving* in a positive direction can have a systemic effect.

Hopeful expectation and the spirited strength of the one-pointed mind can focus the body's energy toward a principle of the right creative relationship to health and happiness, and wellness happens. This is our psychophysical ability to self-heal. It is driven by a personal belief in positive emotions and life-enhancing experiences. Believing in our ability to flourish and enjoying the harmony of life in balance is wellness. The positive psychology of enthusiastic living is powerful medicine. Prayer and affirmation, energized by optimism and faith in a good outcome, are ways to visualize and manifest the healthful, artful life we need and desire. The hope factor can help change and improve our lives by changing and improving our attitude. This *moves* goodwill and positive belief to create health.

Happiness, love, creativity, and hope are natural manifestations of the same essential energy which represent the reliable, old-fashioned medical intangibles that soothe and heal. It's impossible to accurately describe these qualities with data. Science doesn't have a standard measure for the qualitative impacts of the hope factor, or other visceral forms of natural healing. However, it is known that a patient with long-term illness will do better when they have positive emotional relationships and a creative attitude toward life. A wise nurse once told me, "Healing comes from within." The same good source as happiness, love, creativity, and hope.

And as a wise nurse recommends, "Take your Vitamin C-reativity, every day!"

3: Cradle To Grave Creativity

From birth to death, creativity illuminates our thoughts, feelings, and experiences. We are creative beings from conception, through the seasons of time, and until our final breath. Creativity defines the landmarks of our timeline, informing expression from the cradle to grave and bringing emphasis to what counts at life's most important moments. It keeps us relevant at every age and activates the vitality that drives purpose and passion. Experiential creativity makes us healthier, happier, and live longer because it increases cognitive functioning and social engagement which improves our life condition.

Naturally brilliant, a creative brain is essential to good health at every age. It impacts early development, quality of life, and longevity. The brain does more than any other organ. It is the seat of the mind, connected to every bodily function, and a portal of consciousness and unconsciousness. Neuroscientists have made fascinating discoveries over the past decades that offer glimpses into the workings of this three-pound wonder of not so grey matter. Yet, much remains a mystery about how the brain works. Consciously and unconsciously, humans use their entire brain capacity as needed in an energy-efficient manner. The average adult brain has nearly 100 billion neurons, which gives the neuroscientists plenty to study as they explore the curious complexities of our most multifunctional organ.

A creative brain seeks balance, an idea, an emotion. When it is creating, its neurophysiology is similar to learning, praying, healing, or loving. The electrical activity turns on the mind-body experience. The nervous, endocrine, and immune systems work in a symbiotic manner interconnected by a series of neural pathways. Creativity activates this connection and the neurotransmitter dopamine is released. Dopamine is associated with learning, pleasure, reward-seeking behavior, and the activation of creative processes. The release is uplifting and a natural high. It frees inhibitions and activates the sensory flow of perception. Our sense of sight, sound, touch, smell, taste, and intuition are heightened by the brain's mystical dance with creativity. Our senses are intrinsic in how inspiration manifests in the artistic process and how we perceive the experience. The sensory *movement* of creativity is what heals and feels good.

The human brain is wired for creativity. Nearly half of the brain's motor command neurons can mirror what we are feeling and learning in an environment. As well, they can mirror what we see others doing or what they may be feeling. A creative brain is naturally empathic. These sympathetic responses may be linked to how we make our creative mark, the original expression of what we internally think and feel; or our creative match, the observation and interpretation of external experience. In balance, creativity is organically impacted by internal and external responses.

Every brain is unique, slightly asymmetrical with left and right sides. Each side processes information differently. The left side controls speech, language, logic, critical thinking, and technical skills. The right side controls sensory and visual functions, intuition, emotions, free thinking, and creative abilities. The left is linear, intellectual, and rational. It likes facts, rules, and structure. The left brain is the realm of analysis and science. It relates to the past and future. The right side is nonlinear, expressive, and spontaneous. It likes to imagine and break rules without constraints. The right brain is the realm of abstract thinking and art. It relates to being in the present moment. In the brain dance, the left side leads with practical skills as the right side follows with sensory expression, the right feels the desire and the left knows the need. They complement and synergistically *motivate* each other.

Creativity is a balanced brain function that is stimulated in both the left and right regions. Though we tend to have one dominant side, we cannot function solely from a single hemisphere. We need the equilibrium of synapses, both logical and aesthetic, to make creativity happen. The right brain can inspire our brushstrokes, but we need the left brain to technically make them. Emotions are influenced by thoughts and thoughts are influenced by emotions. It takes a bilateral, balanced brain process to write romantic poetry, bake a prize-winning pie, play the piano with gusto, make a compassionate decision, or discover a cure for cancer.

The left and right cerebral hemispheres are connected by the corpus callosum. It is a dense, flat mass of over 200 million neural fibers. This intricate web of wiring is activated throughout our lives and has an important role in transmitting emotions from one region to the other. Neuroplasticity is the brain's capacity to reorganize, rewire, and repair itself by forming new neural connections. We can have a fit creative brain at every age by *motivating* a change in its structure and function in response to experience, sparking neurogenesis. At all stages of life, these synapses generate and regenerate mental abilities and are essential to healthy personal development. We can change our brain by changing our attitude and stimulating the sensory awareness that prompts curiosity and learning.

The mighty human brain works hard and needs to be well stimulated and nourished. It requires the average adult to use approximately 20% of the body's total daily glucose fuel. A developing child's brain uses about 50%. An infant's brain can use up to 60% of their body's life-giving energy. The brain knows what you eat and the quality of the caloric energy put into your body. No fooling the brain. Our smartest organ knows the difference between empty calories and healthful nutrition. It craves an optimal diet that avoids fats, sugars, excessive carbohydrates, and processed foods. Eat smart to be smart.

The brain works like a hologram. It likes to experience new multi-sensory stimuli through creative learning and functioning. This activity benefits the brain relative to our commitment to lifelong learning. The curious and clever brain LOVES to learn. It yearns to learn new things every day. Creative intelligence begins in early childhood when nurtured by parents, our first teachers. Providing children with an interdisciplinary education in the arts and humanities is essential in the twenty-first-century knowledge economy. Creative literacy is more important than IQ for adult successes, such as starting a new business, writing a best-selling book, becoming a respected leader, inventing the next great thing, or being a supportive parent.

Throughout life, we learn from our family, friends, teachers, mentors, environment, and community experience. Lifelong learning is a self-motivated pursuit of knowledge that is passionate and ongoing for personal or professional enrichment. Learning is not confined to the classroom or youth. We learn through investigating an interest and new life experiences. We think, therefore, we can learn at any age. Education studies across the lifespan describe the wellness benefits of creative learning and functioning, and its positive impacts to quality of life and longevity. Research shows the risk of dementia is greatly lowered when people are learning new skills and engaged in meaningful activities. Lifelong learning provides intellectual connectedness in a cultural and social context. As we age, it sparks passion and prompts a sense of purpose. Youngster or oldster, learning supports wellness.

Creativity is a social priority for young people that influences their activities and interests. Healthy self-expression is a hallmark of youth which is supported by education and social systems. Young people need familial participation and mentors who advocate for expressive growth and teach good creative self-care habits. As we grow older, in the decades after age twenty, creative self-care and maintaining a good wellness routine helps balance the stressful issues we confront as we take care of personal and professional responsibilities and the needs of others. "Time" is the resource that most adults have difficulty finding when it comes to self-improvement and self-care. Personal time is essential to wellness. Not having it is an unhealthy dilemma of modern life. Like taking time for brushing your teeth, it is important to establish habits that dedicate time to healthy self-preservation. Investing me-time in wellness pays off over time. DO it for YOU.

Basic creative self-care involves practicing self-expression, eating well and being active, having social support and community interaction, and enjoying restful periods of self-awareness and self-renewal. It's an upgrade to our mind-body-spirit operating system, a reboot and recharge of energy that helps us take control of our circumstances. The process can be a bit untidy and chaotic until we find the balance needed to relax and take care of what really matters. Sometimes, we just need to slow down and keep it simple, one day at a time.

Creative self-care is a kind of intuitive wisdom that nurtures vitality. When we creatively and compassionately care for ourselves it increases energy and self-confidence. It reminds us of our resilience, strength, and grace. Find personal creative sanctuaries and take healing retreats. This could simply be reading for pleasure, a fresh air adventure, taking a dreamy afternoon nap, dinner and a movie, or listening to music. Creative self-care is a healthy habit that improves the quality of life at every age.

When we care for ourselves, we can better care for others. This is true for a large population today as we become caregivers for loved ones during long-term illness or old age and at the end-of-life. In my expressive arts practice and personal life, I've had the privilege to be with people in eldercare, some of whom were near death in hospice or dying at home. The concept of cradle to grave creativity is poignant in the final stages of life and throughout bereavement. Death is as important as birth in the creative continuum of life cycles. Creative doing, communicating, listening, and celebrating are ways to support the dying that includes the caregivers and loved ones in the process. The expressive arts at the end-of-life can facilitate the important things people need to communicate, help with letting go and mending fences, and promote healthy survivorship during and after the experience.

Grieving a death or traumatic loss is an emotional crisis. It is a clinical condition that requires the sufferer to process the pain in stages. It includes denial, anger, bargaining, depression, and finally, acceptance. Grief is not a one-time emotion. It's a personal journey that takes time and self-compassion, and sometimes feeling normal and happy seems like it will never happen. One of life's most poignant emotions, grief reminds us that we love and are loved, and what matters most. Love never leaves, and faith keeps that love forever strong.

The expressive arts are a powerful medium for spiritual healing, celebrating life, sharing hope, and expressing love. Art helps bear witness and unbearable grief. Creative life review through reflecting on personal histories and storytelling can honor a loved one in the present and after passing. End-of-life experiences are transformative times that highlight what is meaningful in life. In the end, when reflecting on our lives, we want to feel that we've made a positive contribution. We all have an inner creative light that animates purpose, kindled by an enduring passion for life.

During my lifetime, and especially in my expressive arts work in hospice, I've met some fascinating older people who seemed to never lose their inner creative light. I am blessed to have had this light shine on me as I witnessed their natural responses to the familiarity of creativity. One amazing light-shining experience happened with two men, both named David, who shared a double-occupancy room in a long-term care facility for patients with advanced dementia. Both men were close to the end-of-life. I had been visiting my hospice friend David with another volunteer for a few weeks, endeavoring to prompt his memory and make him a book from the stories he shared. The illustrated journal was for his wife, who had agreed to participate in the process by painting and printing her hands along with her husband's. The morning we arranged for the hand printing, I arrived and the nurse said, "David, the artist is here." At that moment, the other David who was near death, sat up suddenly in his bed and shouted, "Artists make paintings!" The attending nurse was shocked and amazed at his lively statement because he had been nonverbal and unresponsive for weeks.

What a moment of light! I don't know if he saw the colorful paints in my art basket as he looked at me entering the room, or if it was just hearing the word "artist" that stimulated the deep recall from his broken body. The next week, when I returned to visit my hospice friend David and finish his memory book, the other David's wife and daughter were holding vigil, sweetly singing hymns. With his passing imminent, it was beautiful to see and hear this loving musical tribute. I had learned from his family that he was a retired Unitarian minister, who loved a rousing hymn, and was an accomplished watercolor artist of Maine seascapes. I am grateful to have glimpsed this moment of light at the end of a life, and the beauty and grace of that experience will stay with me, always. Even when the mind and body are done, the creative spirit shines brightly.

Laura Jaquays

4: The Art of Natural Healing

From primitive healers, to modern health and well care systems, humans have practiced medicinal arts in traditional and nontraditional ways. There is wisdom in the healing practices and philosophies of indigenous cultures and our anthropological roots. The art of natural healing enlists our mind-body-spirit energy to create health. It uses the body's remedial powers and holistic therapies to prevent and cure illness. Methods consider the whole well-being of the person, not just the physical body, and that healing is an integrative process. Traditionalists view these diverse healthcare modalities as unconventional, alternative, or complementary. Wellness is a contemporary approach to the art of natural healing.

All life has generative and regenerative capacities to create and recreate, be it human, animal, plant, or microorganism. The healing power of nature, *vis medicatrix naturae*, was the therapeutic philosophy of Hippocrates (460-370 BC), an ancient Greek physician whose doctrine on healing ethics is still in use today. The Hippocratic Oath states, "If I keep this oath faithfully, may I enjoy my life and practice my art, respected by all humanity in all times." Hippocrates considered healing to be an art, and that the essential function of the physician is to never do harm, and to avoid treatment that interferes with the body's natural processes to create health.

For millennia, holistic practitioners from indigenous cultures have used artistic tools to aid healing. Cave paintings are the earliest forms of recorded art in human history. Often these images were created by the shaman, the first artist-healer, who would use natural and supernatural methods to lead the tribe to health. The shaman can be a tribal elder, a medicine man or woman, or a high priest or priestess. Generally, it's an individual who has experienced their own miraculous healing in a way that endows them with special knowledge and the skills to lead others to health and well-being. A guardian of the healing and cultural traditions of the tribe, the shaman is entrusted to preserve and pass them on to the next generation. The shaman uses a treasure trove of creative mediums in combination with elements from nature. A shamanic ceremony is a highly sensory experience. Adorned with tools and talismans, the shaman wears symbolic regalia with a headdress or mask. Art, dance, music, stories, and medicinal herbs are used in rituals that focus positive intention toward the healing remedy needed. Prayers, chants, and sounds from drums, rattles, flutes, and zithers transport the experience with rhythmic vibration. Humor is a transformational tool in the arts medicine bag that metaphorically complements the process.

Sand paintings are created in many aboriginal and indigenous cultures. The artwork represents various types of circular designs that are made from earth and natural materials. In the Navajo tradition, they are made by the medicine man for healing purposes to treat physical and emotional illness. It is made on the floor of the patient's home or wherever the healing ceremony takes place. The painting is tinted with natural pigments in colors sacred to the tribe. It illustrates a particular order and symmetry symbolic of the harmony desired by the patient, who sits in the image like a portal. The medicine man uses herbs, prayer, and rhythmic movement to summon the Holy People to assist in the healing ritual. When the ceremony is done, the sand painting is destroyed because it is now considered toxic having absorbed the illness from the patient, who is ultimately responsible for their own recovery. Like any healing remedy, the patient must have faith in the healer and their own capacity to achieve health.

The Native American Medicine Wheel symbolically represents a nonlinear model of human development. From ancient times, indigenous people have developed it as a spiritual paradigm for health, education, and storytelling. The circular design reflects there are no straight lines in nature. Round patterns mirror the interconnectedness of all life and the cosmos. They represent the elements and seasons, the cycles of time, and birth, adulthood, death, and rebirth. It's a wheel of energy that is eternally in *motion* - east, south, west, and north, below and above - in all directions in harmony with the flow of nature. The Medicine Wheel is a sacred circle representing the universal life force, known in the Lakota way of life as *Wakan Tanka*, or *The Great Everything*. The circular design has four parts that represent the mind, body, heart, and spirit, with a center space marking the axis of the Self and Creator. The concept embraces wellness as the standard for living in balance with nature in relationship to self, others, and the Universe.

Medicine wheels are created using various art forms. There are ancient sites where the remnants of giant circular structures built from rocks and stone cairns have endured. These landmarks of art and nature were used for community rituals and the purposes of counting time and charting the stars. The medicine wheel is a cultural symbol in the arts, literature, and history. A circle marking the four directions is a common artistic image that embellishes pottery, baskets, visual art, and sculpture. It is an enduring and powerful symbol that teaches us what goes around comes around, and how the energy we put out, good or bad, comes back full circle, and that we must live in balance with all life and the cycles of nature.

The circle is a powerful image for optimal health and personal equipoise. It is a centering symbol for wholeness, a point for starting and arriving. Without a beginning or end, the form is a continuous flow of energy in *motion*. As humans evolved, with our developing brain, eyes, and a tool in hand, the round shape was one of the first images we made. Primordially, we naturally use a single finger to create the circumference. There are artifacts worldwide of circles that humans crafted, built, scribed, painted, or carved. The singular circle manifested as a symbol for the perfection of God that is everywhere, in everyone, and in all time and space.

The mandala is a circular symbol for wholeness and the interconnectedness of all life. Mandala is the Sanskrit word for a sacred circle. In Tibetan Buddhist culture, a mandala is an artistic tool for spiritual meditation and transformation that guides the individual to gain wisdom and compassion along the path to enlightenment. The circle is naturally part of personal symbology. Like a wheel, it *moves* and evolves through the ups and downs of life, navigating the smooth and bumpy dimensions of our existence and keeping the energetic life force humming along. The geometric shape engenders focused attention and balance.

Psychologists report that people engaged in art therapy can spontaneously create mandala-like drawings that represent the unconscious aspects in their life that lack integration with the conscious mind. Drawing a mandala focuses attention and directs the chaos of thoughts and emotions. It fosters deep contemplation and relaxation. Sometimes intersected by a square, the harmonious shape helps visualize whole well-being. Mandala therapy mirrors the subtle changes we need for the outcomes we desire and creates a healthy symbol for emotional balance. As a personal art form, it can be a reminder of our creative potential and resilience.

The art of natural healing is part of every culture and stage of life. From the cradle to the grave, it supports our body's natural ability to create health. It is a way to wellness that improves our daily routines and gives meaning to what we value most. Creative therapies in a nurturing environment are ways to care for our mind, body, spirit, and emotions. Art and natural elements integrated into a medical protocol significantly benefits the healing process.

Florence Nightingale (1820-1910) was an English medical and social reformer. A practicing nurse, she recognized that patients who were suffering did better when they had sunlight and could see the colors of nature through a window. A trailblazer in modern nursing, she led a social crusade to improve the sanitary conditions of hospitals and quality of public healthcare. She was an activist who advocated for compassionate care and a holistic approach that considered the wellness of the patient from a humanistic perspective. Nurses are on the front lines of healthcare. Most often, they are the nurturing force that offers loving kindness and healing hands to comfort patients.

Another holistic pioneer, Edwin D. Babbitt (1828-1907) was a leading American practitioner and writer in the field of color research and chromotherapy. He treated a range of mental and physical health problems with light reflected through colored glass. Believing in the healing qualities of color and light, he invented the chromolume, a device with colored lenses that are activated by natural light sources. Designed like a window, it was a popular home decor item in the Victorian era. Many grand homes featured a chromolume in a sitting room or stairwell window, positioned to allow the natural light and colored reflections affect mood and general well-being. With his early and innovative concepts of wellness, Babbitt used the natural healing capacities of color and light to create healthful environments and self-care tools for his patients.

Today, the arts, nature, and many forms of ambient color and light are used in health and wellness settings to promote a comfortable, stress-free experience for patients, caregivers, visitors, and the medical staff. Studies show when a patient feels safe and relaxed in a healthcare environment, they can more effectively cope with medical interventions and require less medication for anxiety and pain. The arts complement clinical care and provide sensory qualities that enhance the healing campus of a hospital. It includes natural lighting, green spaces, sculpture gardens, and visual arts or music in public areas. Hospitals increase the quality of care and improve patient experience when they provide wellness support.

The expressive arts involve an individual or group process in a clinical or non-clinical setting. They are participatory mediums that naturally build on each other while fostering personal growth and a sense of community. The experiential process nurtures confidence and skills for continued development. Expressive arts involve multimodal approaches within psychology, health and wellness, education, and community arts. There is a palette of possibilities in the emerging field of medical humanities involving participatory arts and creative interventions that include visual arts, dance, music, writing, humor, improvisation, drama, and elements of play. These activities cultivate the individual's natural creative abilities and bring peer groups together in a shared community experience.

The role of the expressive arts therapist or practitioner is to facilitate a safe environment that supports creativity in an individual or group process. The facilitator guides participants through a creative medium that engages and opens them to self-expression and self-discovery. The process teaches skills for better understanding needs and communicating feelings through a creative self-care practice that can be enjoyed ongoing. Creativity supports both the physical and emotional aspects of an illness. Acute or chronic disease can be a recalibration of energy that impacts physical identity while opening new awareness to emotional strengths and resilience. Prescriptive creativity is customized to cultivate interests and personal expression.

The expressive arts differ from art therapy in that the process engenders a spontaneous, self-directed experience. Artistic mediums support physical and psychological needs while focusing on personal talents and skill-building. These methods are integrative when used in combination with clinical treatment. Traditional art therapy takes a more psychological approach that follows a diagnosis and treatment model. They are both valued by science and participants. The expressive arts engage the actual phenomenon and *movement* of the creative experience as wellness therapy. Whatever the modality, when using art to support healing, the facilitator should not over-interpret a participant's outcome or offer a linear judgment of a nonlinear process. Creative therapies should be open and fluid with more encouragement than evaluation.

Natural arts-based therapies in medicine have strong links between research and practice. There are positive outcomes at every level of application in healthcare. Overall, therapies improve emotional well-being and significantly reduce stress. Evaluation methods take into account quantitative and qualitative data based on physiological and psychological impacts. They are recorded through direct participant interviews and feedback, written surveys, staff reports, and anecdotal observation. Applying statistical measures to a multidimensional experience is useful information for analyzing outcomes and developing new programs. However, the alchemy of a creative healing experience cannot be explained by data. The best evidence is how it makes people feel and the meaningful ways it enriches their daily lives.

The expressive arts are on the forefront of a new age of humanistic medicine that values a patient-centered approach to care and the fundamental principles of open communication and mutual respect between physician and patient. As we overhaul and reinvent healthcare, these positive qualities will become a new standard in medicine. Beginning with education, top medical schools are requiring arts and humanities courses for doctors to help them better observe and communicate with their patients, and to manage the high levels of stress associated with getting a medical degree. Both the practitioner and the patient benefit from creative engagement and enrichment.

The expressive arts began with the ancients and are being redefined today, as the best wellness practices become integrated into healthcare and accessible to a larger population. In the first half of the twentieth century, arts-based therapies were recognized through the groundbreaking work of Carl Gustav Jung (1875-1961). A Swiss psychiatrist and psychoanalyst, he was the founder of modern psychology and a hands-on healing practitioner, spiritual philosopher, and new age mystic. His approach involved the concept of individuation, a theory that applies the psychological process of integrating opposites to become a whole being by recognizing conscious and unconscious archetypes. Jung is known for his research and writing about personality types and scientific contributions to dream analysis and symbolization. The Jungian theory of the collective unconscious suggests there is a universal psychic system that is unconscious and impersonal, yet, it is identical and connected in all living forms. The preeminent practitioner of expressive arts, he wrote, as early as 1916 and throughout his career until his death, about his preferred method of arts-based psychotherapy.

Jungian methods combined visual art, movement, sound, drama, and storytelling. Creative visualization, dreamwork, yoga, and writing were the healing protocols he prescribed to patients and practiced privately. He believed that creativity relieved stress and anxiety, helped express emotional trauma, and was an integrative medium in the nonlinear process of individuation. A natural practitioner, Jung advocated the transformative power of art. He encouraged his patients to practice creative self-care. Like a shaman, he used creative therapies customized for the self-actualization and self-healing of the patient. Jung conceived a theory of active imagination. He described it as the inborn creative process and dynamic mode of inquiry that *moves* and personifies expression. Today, the expressive arts model Jungian theories, and are evolved to include less technical analysis and more experiential processes designed to engage an individual's natural healing capacities.

The expressive arts are multimodal therapeutic practices that happen in a clinical or non-clinical setting, with a trained therapist in a group or one-to-one process, or simply through maintaining a creative self-care practice. Art-making, art-taking, and art-giving are ready remedies in the medicine bag. In my professional and personal experience, I've learned the practical applications and appreciate how these beneficial practices have improved every aspect of my life. Medicine, in its highest purpose, is the science and art of natural healing. A healer is someone who gives you confidence in your vitality and ability to self-heal. From the shaman and indigenous healing traditions, to modern prescriptive creativity and the evolving field of expressive arts, to just doing the creative things we love to do - art naturally heals.

5: Dr. Creativity

Creativity activates the inner physician. On-call 24/7, 365 days a year, whether sick or well, Dr. Creativity provides ready remedies for improving health and well-being. Creative wellness education and therapies benefit individuals and communities in the workplace, schools, and healthcare.

The information in this chapter is a broad brushstroke illustrating how prescriptive creativity supports wellness. There is no single method or delivery system. What I offer is not a comprehensive guide. It's a reference that highlights the practical applications and positive potential for health. Seekers and practitioners are encouraged to explore and learn more about creative healing opportunities by participating in the process and becoming active in community initiatives.

It starts with a story. We all have biological and historical stories to tell. Storytelling *moves* creative energy to stimulate healing through expressing our thoughts, feelings, and experiences in narrative mediums. This common therapy is important in the relationship between every patient and healthcare provider. Being able to communicate and relate your story to a doctor can help them better prescribe the appropriate treatments. Personal narrative in medicine reveals the human condition, and what we learn from these stories improves healthcare communication and our ability to understand and cure illness.

Through telling and listening to stories, we can make sense of our lives and tap an instinctive process to naturally create health. The practice of writing a personal narrative helps control blood pressure and levels of stress which can balance the need for more prescription medication. Narrative therapy includes oral or written storytelling and poetry, keeping a journal, contributing to a blog, and writing with a group. Visual arts, music, improvisation, and performance are other forms of narrative language. Storytelling and narrative therapies support patient well care with the hands on support of social workers and therapists.

People suffering from mental health or behavioral disorders benefit from creative processes that help them develop self-care tools for managing emotions and the debilitating symptoms caused by genetic and environmental factors. Expressive arts and prescriptive creativity support treatment for depression, chemical addictions, obsessive compulsive disorder (OCD), attention-deficit hyperactivity disorder (ADHD), schizophrenia, autism, dementia, seasonal affective disorder (SAD), common learning disabilities like dyslexia, and a range of psychological and behavioral conditions. Through the arts, personal ideas and emotions can be expressed in cognitive and physical ways.

Natural creative therapies are a healthier way to foster emotional resiliency and coping methods, versus the more common psychopharmacological approach of prescribing drugs, and only the minimal "talk time" for patients with a psychotherapist. Creativity helps people who are at an emotional threshold in life. Whether guided by a therapist or in a self-care practice, the expressive arts build personal communication and coping skills, promote self-confidence, nurture a positive perspective, and reduce stress. The arts are a way to connect when feeling disconnected.

Expressive arts are beneficial in recovery therapy for individuals suffering from post-traumatic stress disorder (PTSD). People who suffer from PTSD include survivors of traumatic brain injury (TBI), emotional or physical abuse, violence, war, terrorism, and natural disasters. Sufferers can address stress, fear, and anger through creative coping and resiliency methods. Storytelling is an effective medium for communicating what is difficult to express through ordinary language. It can put traumatic events into perspective and give people a place to put their trauma. Creative engagement helps trauma sufferers safely free the pain that is locked in the subconscious through a conscious expressive process. To liberate it by living it. To embody and befriend the memory, and be able to trust the present moment and others.

The mental and emotional dissociation caused by trauma lives in the physical body. Until it can be released, it can be profoundly debilitating. Scientists are finding evidence how the devastating effects of traumatic events are imprinted in the body, both psychologically and physically. Trauma can disembody the mind and spirit, and detach the sufferer from their natural resilience and power. The effects of stress from trauma negatively impacts the adrenal system and functions connected to fight or flight responses. It neurologically impairs the body which responds with panic attacks, extreme anxiety, and the feeling of being out of control and an outsider. For PTSD sufferers, the mindfulness of creativity helps relieve depression and improves self-confidence. It provides a redemptive capacity supported by a safe environment that nurtures a healthy sense of purpose and connection.

Arts-based therapies benefit people who suffer from secondary trauma and those who work with or are close to others who've experienced severe trauma. This includes emergency first responders, law enforcement, the military, healthcare workers who care for critically ill patients, and empathic individuals who help people in crisis. Creative self-care helps the survivor of a tragic event who is crippled by the guilt of having survived when others did not. Over the long term, treating trauma with art interventions can be highly effective, often when clinical methods have failed. They provide a PTSD sufferer with a way to balance emotional responses, maintain a positive attitude, and find a sustainable path to recovery.

Creativity can be heightened by post-traumatic growth when a trauma empowers personal expression and prompts self-actualization in ways that are profoundly transformative and healing. It is beneficial behavior that springs from adversity and unleashes the individual's strengths and gifts. It sparks hope and the desire to create a new and better life.

An example of post-traumatic growth is Malala Yousafzai (1997-), the Pakistani activist for the human rights and education of women and youngest-ever Nobel Prize laureate. In 2012 at age 15, she was shot by the Taliban on her way to school in a violent attempt to silence her outspoken advocacy for women. Malala survived the attack and inspired an international campaign for her cause that has raised awareness and won her deserved recognition and numerous awards for human rights. A traumatic experience can have a healing impact that *moves* life's obstacles into benefactors. It can become an impetus to create positive change, personally and for the greater good. Beyond unspeakable events, a life trauma can be a call to speak with creative true voice that informs and inspires.

Creative activity benefits mental health. It helps balance emotional conflicts and minimizes self-destructive behaviors. The process focuses attention and promotes a sense of identity and stability. We should never prioritize our physical health over mental health. Clinical depression has debilitating symptoms that affect overall health, including suppression of the immune system, too much or a lack of sleep, poor concentration and low energy, changes in appetite, feelings of worthlessness, and negative thoughts that are sometimes suicidal. It's a medical condition, not a personality trait, that affects the brain with the abnormal functioning of the vital neurotransmitters serotonin, norepinephrine, and dopamine. Depression and anxiety substantially increase cortisol, the stress hormone.

Art is a connecting factor and self-empowerment tool for gaining what is lost to the malaise of depression. As a complementary therapy, in addition to personalized talk-time with a psychotherapist, it can minimize the need for prescription drugs. Anxiety disorders are the most common mental illness in the United States, affecting more than 20% of the adult population. Highly treatable, yet, only about a third of those suffering receive therapy, and many individuals are undiagnosed. Relatively common, though there is nothing common about suffering from depression. Ultimately, the individual needs to find a balance with clinical treatment, emotional support from peers, and extreme self-care to maintain homeostasis. During this difficult process, creativity is a way to nurture self-awareness and self-preservation.

The expressive arts are important for at-risk youth who are negatively impacted by social, psychological, and physical factors. Music in combination with visual or written expression and performative arts can reduce anxiety levels in adolescents who demonstrate negative social behavior. It gives them a sense of voice, place, and purpose. Music is a powerful medium for communication that relates to peer culture and individualism. The ability to engage in the arts and make healthy social connections prevents youth from associating with negative behavior that leads to addiction, delinquency, and troubles in adulthood. Art therapy helps manage stress and difficult relationships. Increasing numbers of teens are being treated for anxiety and depression. Schools and community groups that offer creative wellness and mindfulness programs are important resources for youth. They nurture social confidence and inclusion in all aspects of life. These activities provide a safe place for creativity in a peer setting and help young people develop skills for positive growth and resilience.

ADHD is the acronym for Attention Deficit Hyperactivity Disorder. It's a psychiatric diagnosis for young people often described as a dysfunction. Unfortunately, there can be a rush to medicalize the condition and treat it with psycho-stimulants. Neuroscience shows that people with ADHD are hard-wired for novelty-seeking behavior. It is a positive trait that drives creative curiosity and innovation. People with ADHD are generally bored and want to focus on their interests. Over-stimulation from external sources, like digital technology, can worsen the condition. The behavior doesn't fit the expectations of education and contemporary culture, so it is suppressed with medication.

A child with ADHD is more likely to respond to out-of-the-box creative thinking and learning. When engaged, they can have a laser-like focus doing what they love to do. This quality helps advance achievements in art and science. Over-medication is counterintuitive. A child aware of their diagnosis may feel stigmatized with what is perceived as a defect early in life. A young lifetime of medications, like those used to treat ADHD, can inhibit sensory and creative abilities and be a path to medicating behaviors in adulthood. Physical hyper-activeness and contrary behaviors are managed with daily medication. It helps the people around the child and could be the only way to control how they act and learn in social environments. We need to understand ADHD, and use fewer chemical interventions and more of what is positive about this behavior. Engaging the child in project-focused creative learning methods engenders a sense of connection and provides opportunities for personal successes in the classroom and beyond. Mindfulness techniques are currently used in schools to help ADHD students focus attention and learn positive habits for social and emotional growth.

Visual art helps children with autism focus attention and model what they see. It stimulates the motor skills and emotional expression impaired by their condition. I have worked with young people who are learning and occupationally disabled to an extreme degree. It requires the facilitation of daily activities and education by their parents, counselors, and teachers. I teach fresh-air watercolor classes in Maine. One summer afternoon, a mother and her son made a deep impression on me by demonstrating how immediate the process of art-making can relax the sometimes intense behavior of autism. Jason, an autistic teenager, arrived at the class physically agitated and screaming. This behavior was related to his condition, making it difficult for his mother to cope. She confessed how she was looking forward to my class and a little wellness time for herself while on vacation. The boy was more than a handful, and she needed a break.

Other teens were painting in the class. I demonstrated a basic watercolor technique, gave Jason a brush, and nudged him to go for it. His mother was getting into the process and decided to copy one of my seascapes. Jason also followed this model, and we were able to keep him happy, quiet, and engaged for over an hour. When he was done he announced it. Then he calmly picked up his incredibly accurate rendering of my visual model and waited for his mother. She disclosed to me, throughout the class, about the stress of caring for her only child, and how it was important to be able to paint and relax. In tears of gratitude, Jason's mother left the class with a goal to get her watercolors out of the box where she had stored them for the past 20 years, and promised to make creative self-care time for herself that also benefits her son. This is creative wellness in action.

Music-based therapies prompt autistic children to identify feelings such as happy, sad, or scary, which are emotions they sometimes cannot understand without musical intervention. Musical savants are rare individuals who often have severe autism and lack the emotional capacity to function normally, though they can play music brilliantly. Sometimes a gifted savant will memorize a complicated work of music after having heard it only a single time. They can then play it with a high degree of musical intelligence and skill, often repeating the music to an extreme. Music creates the power to improvise and release emotions. It is often a stabilizing therapy for dealing with the communication obstacles associated with many forms of autism.

Music therapy improves many aspects of health and daily living. The well-documented physical and cognitive benefits of music experience are stress reduction, immune system support, improved breathing and vitality, heart rate stabilization, and pain reduction. The emotional and social benefits are self-expression, self-awareness, and connection to others. Music is a vibrational medicine that we hear and feel. It is the most accessible and immediately therapeutic medium of all the expressive arts. The *movement* of musical rhythm is naturally part of our sound creative wellness.

Life can be unstructured and disordered, whereas music is structured and ordered. The brain recognizes music as an emotional diversion and a form of *motion*. Music activates the areas of the brain associated with empathy and learning; though this multidimensional organ has no singular musical part. Multiple brain regions and the senses are activated when making or listening to music. It engages visual, auditory, and motor functions. Music affects fundamental aspects of brain function including language, the experience of perception, and our ability to process complex sequences.

Music as medicine was practiced and well-documented since ancient times. Science is still working to measure the healthful aspects of music and its impacts on the human condition. It is reported that the scientists studying music and the brain are enjoying their research and listening. Not surprising because many scientists play musical instruments. More and more, research shows the brain's responses to music have positive effects on health and well-being. Science will likely discover that music is a naturally healing remedy for many negative conditions that plague humanity.

The balanced brain responds to music through motor and sensory functions with the linguistic, technical, rhythmic left side in harmony with the expressive, feeling, improvisational right side. Music is vibrational energy, similar to the varying rhythms of nature. Music alters brainwave patterns and levels of stress hormones in the bloodstream producing the balance needed for homeostasis. The remedy goes to the need. As a healing function, music directly impacts the body vibrationally with immediate and ongoing effects. Our responses are positive or negative, depending on sound quality, volume, rhythm, and lyric content. Each of us reacts uniquely to music, and the memory of music, relative to personal preferences and how it makes us feel.

For people handicapped with a disability, music and movement supports emotional and physical challenges. Performative arts offer empowering opportunities for self-expression that helps people feel less disenfranchised and more connected to themselves and others. They are a validation of the body that greatly improves the quality of life. The transformational dynamic of music and movement stimulates the mind-body-spirit experience. It engenders self-confidence and a physical assurance that measurably affects mobility affliction and affords a dignified experience.

Parkinson's Disease is a progressive neurodegenerative movement disorder, the hallmark indicator being the lack of dopamine production in the brain. It results in debilitating symptoms that cause tremors, muscle rigidity, mobility problems, and difficulty balancing. When engaged in dance and music, Parkinson's patients can orient themselves through a rhythmic activity to improve balance and stability. The exertion helps override the feeling that the disease is in control. Music, dance, and many forms of hands-on making or crafting help focus the mind and body. These activities relieve pain and muscle stiffness and build strength while promoting social connection, personal accomplishment, and well-being. I've worked with Parkinson's patients who could *move* a paintbrush to make an image without hand tremors. Typically, the shaking makes a simple gesture nearly impossible. The rhythmic *movement* of expression stimulates the brain-eyes-hands function and helps balance neurological affliction.

Stroke and traumatic brain injury recovery involve various types of occupational therapy to help regain the loss of physical and mental functioning due to a neurological crisis. Mood, memory, concentration, and motor skills are impacted. During recovery, arts-based therapies activate the damaged areas of the brain with positive sensory stimuli. They promote learning and recall, increase physical coordination, and support well-being.

Music can vibrationally reactivate the brain after a stroke. This *movement* helps the victim regain cognitive abilities. Therapies that engage the eyes and hands to prompt the brain functions include drawing, crafting, tinkering, making, and playing. The use of video games and digital devices develops the brain-eyes-hands dexterity that helps stroke victims recover damaged functions. Technology provides a one-dimensional medium that simplifies and aids the process. Making and looking at visual art, making and listening to music, and dance and low-impact exercise are multidimensional mediums that build neurological and physical capacities, improve communication, and provide sensory enrichment.

The inspiring story of the American neuroanatomist Dr. Jill Bolte Taylor (1959-) is evidence of the brain's brilliance and resilience. At age 37, the scientist gained creative insight when she suffered a massive brain hemorrhage. In her case, she was conscious and vividly aware of how one half of the brain goes into action to accommodate the loss of the other side's malfunction due to a stroke. The stroke was happening in her intellectual, left brain hemisphere while she could discern that her emotional, right brain was taking control of her actions and perception. The profound insight caused by the stroke was a new understanding of the right brain's ability to perceive beauty, euphoria, and empathy. Her right brain activated a highly conscious multi-sensory feeling, an expansive sensation she described as Nirvana, a state of bliss. After the stroke, she had a heightened sense of color and visual creativity that inspired her to make stained-glass art as a therapy. Today, Dr. Jill is an author, educator, and leader in helping others recover from neurological trauma, and she raises awareness of the amazing human brain's healing qualities.

Sometimes, the trauma of a stroke rewires and reengineers the brain in ways that open the victim to new talents while having no memories of others. This also happens with Alzheimer's Disease. Suddenly, creative expression is unblocked by changes in the brain in profound ways, waking up one part of cognition while another closes down. When art becomes a basic impulse that is not affected by neurological degeneration, individuals may demonstrate an expressive skill that they never used before the disease, like painting pictures. Familiar art, music, films, photographs, and stories stimulate memory, and can be sensory references for helping dementia patients connect time and place with meaning.

Unfortunately, in the case of Alzheimer's, eventually the disease wins the battle. Alzheimer's disease is a progressive brain disorder characterized by deterioration of mental faculties resulting from the loss of nerve cells and the connections between them. It causes a build-up of plaque in the hippocampus, an area of the brain that functions as the central hard-drive of memory. The symptoms of this form of dementia include memory loss, confusion, anxiety, and sleep disorders. It can progress from mild to severe in a relatively short time. There is no effective medical treatment for the disease, yet, evidence points to the caregiver's support role as being the key to maintaining some degree of functioning. Memory certainly matters, so a family member or friend can share what is familiar to prompt recall.

Creative interventions that involve memory and social interaction help manage symptoms and keep communication channels open. Music is particularly effective in prompting memory, and in some cases, it seems like a miracle. Better than more medications that numb sensitivity, music activates the senses and engages dementia suffers in an enjoyable experience that reminds them of their old selves and the rhythms of life. Listening to music and the memory of familiar music is old-fashioned medicine.

The expressive arts are supportive to patients during long-term illness and at the end-of-life, as well as their families and caregivers. Grief is a clinical condition and one of our deepest emotions. It suppresses the immune system and causes depression and anxiety. Palliative and hospice care are difficult in any health dynamic. Here again, the expressive arts improve the quality of life in meaningful ways that highlight what's important, to help the individual let go and be at peace. Visual art, writing memories, reading poetry, and listening to music are ways to comfort grieving and bear witness during the end-of-life. Music played for someone near death or in a comatose state is still vibrationally sensed. Even at this threshold of unconsciousness, the rhythmic qualities are experienced. As well, a deaf individual can respond to sounds they vibrationally feel but can't hear.

Cancer patients use expressive arts to help cope with the symptoms of their illness and bouts of depression that can be a side-effect of the disease. A cancer diagnosis requires the patient to practice extreme self-care for what is often a long and difficult treatment. Arts-based therapies strengthen self-identity, reduce stress, and promote physical and emotional well-being. Origami, a classic paper folding method, is a good hands-on activity for people receiving chemotherapy because it focuses the mind and relieves treatment-related neuropathy, a condition which causes numbness in the fingers or other extremities. Creative expression aids the disorienting symptoms of chemo-brain which affects patients while in chemotherapy, making it difficult to do basic tasks such as speak, concentrate, and remember. Expressive arts workshops offer a supportive process for people with cancer or other chronic illness by helping them connect with peers, friends, and community members.

My role as an expressive arts facilitator is to nurture the natural healing capacities of creativity, teach new skills, and support participants by giving them confidence in their abilities. In one-to-one sessions or groups, I try to spark their process, and gently guide them through ways to start and maintain a creative practice. In a group workshop, there is the benefit of input from peers. Through my work with wellness support groups for cancer and other long-term illness, I've experienced firsthand the value of participatory arts in a group. There is creative empowerment in social ecology for the individual and collective. The healing power of a group gives a communal perspective of being outside ourselves and part of a greater existence. It's me to we, the emergence of the individual within a peer community. The interaction of creativity and spontaneity enlivens the process and *motivates* participants to be present in a sensory experience with others.

Through a collective experience, we have opportunities to collaborate in ways that help us trust others, bear witness, and *move* our energy toward a creative goal together. Group arts encourage listening, looking, learning, and sharing. They are a fusion of common interests and comfort. The interactive and participatory dynamics of a peer group provides a safe sense of belonging and connectedness.

Health and wellness organizations are clinical resources that provide community-based venues to support therapeutic arts for people living with chronic illness. Expressive arts programs in non-clinical settings include special events, workshops, and retreats at cultural venues or natural locations accessible to the general public. Getting together with people to *move* and share an artistic process can be a peak creative experience - a moment when we are doing an expressive activity with others in a transformative social interaction.

Dr. Creativity is in the house! For individuals and communities, the expressive arts are a ready remedy in the medicine bag.

Part Two: Creative Wellness Model

6: A Model for Creative Living

Being creative is about being YOU. Everyone expresses creativity in unique ways. Many daily activities are creative, from home to hobby to work to community. Everyday creativity is the way to express originality and bring meaning to life. Our diverse personalities, lifestyles, and interests are sources of creative self-expression, a multiverse of possibilities easily tapped. Our remarkable capacity for creative thinking, doing, and being is what makes us human. Every aspect of daily surviving and thriving is a way to healthful, artful living.

Creativity happens and wellness is activated when we are art-making, *the experience of creating*, art-taking, *experiencing what is created*, and art-giving, *sharing a creative experience*. It's experiential whether we are just thinking about it, engaged in hands-on originating and ordinary tasks, or involved in the collective culture. Creativity is a positive growth mindset. It complements our hierarchy of needs to help us reach our highest potential and happiest homeostasis. Being present in the moment of the process is why it is so satisfying and beneficial to health and well-being. This important human quality supports every stage of personal development and enriches how we grow and stay *motivated* to create our best life.

How are you creative? Knowing and doing your creativity is the way to wellness. Consider the creative things you love to do and the ways you naturally express yourself every day. Take a personal inventory. Include the peak creative experiences that say, "I am creative." Identify what you have done, are doing, and want to do. Who and what are your co-creators? When and where do you create? How do you express thoughts and feelings? What is your creative wellness? Recognizing creativity empowers daily activities and makes common things un-common. Understanding and appreciating your creative talents and abilities increases enjoyment in every aspect of living.

What is creative living? Everyone requires a creative life to survive and thrive as individuals and communities. Creativity supports basic needs and celebrates the things that matter most. From the cradle to the grave, creative living is a con-scious way of creating a life in balance. Like seekers throughout the ages, I've explored many dimensions of creativity. Through my observations and musings, I've identified the common ways people are creative. Informed by decades of teaching creative wellness and my lifetime of artistic practice and curiosity, I've developed a model for creative living. It's an organic approach designed to activate creative thinking, doing, and being; and *motivate* your purpose, passion, and practice. It is a self-em-powerment tool for self-actualization and self-expression that suggests a unified creativity theory. Bound by my artist-who-loves-science imagination, I've organized the model in a series of narrative algorithms and essays. Together, the positive phi-losophy explodes the myth that any human could ever be un-creative. We are all creative. Life is creative.

To facilitate the big picture of this idea and begin a big-ger conversation, I've developed the *ART HOPE Creative Well-ness Model*. It is a universal application for everyday creativity that relates to our personal life and interests, workplace, educa-tion, healthcare, corporations, and communities and leadership, locally and globally. The concept represents the many ways people are creative. It highlights mental, physical, spiritual, envi-ronment, community, home, language, sound, and visual as-pects. These nine themes are interconnected and suggest the organic potential of creativity. Most of us can relate to some in-terest or activity in each aspect of the model. Use it as an idea catcher to spark creativity, prompt an interest or hobby, and help identify opportunities for expression.

The nine aspects illustrate a basic model for creative living. **MENTAL**, **PHYSICAL**, and **SPIRITUAL** relate to the mind-body-spirit connection. This is our creative thinking, doing, and being, the experiential trinity inherent in all creative processes. **ENVIRONMENT, COMMUNITY**, and **HOME** relate to belonging and a sense of place. **LANGUAGE, SOUND**, and **VISUAL** relate to the expression of thoughts and feelings. **Love** is the universal energy that inspires and *motivates* our creativity. We need all these aspects in a healthy balance.

Creativity is impossible to compartmentalize. It is interactive, a generative and regenerative energy that permeates all of life. The model represents dynamics that are changing and in *motion*. When applied, the aspects are interrelated and interchangeable and reflect commonalities we all share. Creativity isn't limited to the model because it's fluid and fundamental.

Diverse aspects of creativity blend into our everyday experience. For example, you can take a walk (physical) with a friend (community) in a park (environment) while hearing birds sing (sound) as you tell a good story (language) about making cupcakes (home) that were whimsically decorated (visual). Of course, your original thought (mental) created this special experience that warmed your heart with joy (spiritual). That's healthy fun and all the aspects of creative wellness in one afternoon!

As you explore themes, the question at the end of each essay prompts personal reflection and response. Draw, write, or use mixed media, and take your creativity off the page to make a personal inventory of how you are creative. What you learn about yourself can become a foundation for being the artist-in-residence in your very creative life. Make it your masterpiece!

ART HOPE Creative Wellness Model
Aspects of Everyday Creativity

Recognize and practice everyday creativity. Apply the model to your lifestyle, interests, and what you love and value. Creativity is the way to wellness and healthful, artful living.

MENTAL

creative thinking, the *moving* mind, reasoning, imagination, learning, innovation, problem-solving, tinkering, STEAM, information, applied knowledge, technology, technical skill, contemplation, sensory awareness, mindfulness, dreaming

PHYSICAL

creative doing, physical *movement*, sensory response, expression **art**iculated, self-care, play, sex, home chores, fitness, sports, human-powered activities, rhythm, dance, making music, mind-body-spirit exercise, what *moves* you

SPIRITUAL

creative being, Creator-creature connection, prayer, spirituality, hope factor, religious groups and services, sacred symbols, illumination arts, sentient nature, holy ground, meditation, ritual, peak creative experience, emotions in *motion*, love

ENVIRONMENT

Earth consciousness, environmental stewardship, habitat, being in nature, having a vista, color, light, circadian rhythms, seasons and cycles, atmospheric activities, everyday environs, personal space, creative ecosystems, travel, special places

COMMUNITY

social sphere, art of relationship, family, partners, pets, friends, neighbors, colleagues, fellowship, groups, organizations, diversity, your tribe, fashion, public venues, social networks, citizen artist, volunteering, activism, community arts, celebration

HOME

artist-in-residence, living space, sense of place, native habitat, homesteading, homemaking, domestic arts, shelter in place, organizing, interior design, home improvement, home office, hobbies, handicrafts, gardening, cooking, creative refuge

LANGUAGE

internal or external language, verbal or written communication, sensory mediums, speaking, listening, gesturing, vernacular, media, narrative, storytelling, words, reading, writing, imagery, symbols, emoticons, humor, dreams, creative affirmations

SOUND

hearing or feeling sound, mechanical wave energy, resonance, sound memory, rhythmic vibration, soundscapes, silence, sound nutrition, nature's song, vocal and instrumental music, music therapy, deep listening, spoken language, mantras

VISUAL

look to see to remember to enjoy, observation, point of view, brain-eyes-hands function, making or seeing visual art, drawing, painting, photography, video, chromotherapy, color, light, rainbow code, internal or external imagery, creative visualization

7: Mental Creative Wellness

creative thinking, the *moving* mind, reasoning, imagination,
learning, innovation, problem-solving, tinkering, STEAM,
information, applied knowledge, technology, technical skill,
contemplation, sensory awareness, mindfulness, dreaming

Creativity is mental. In *motion*, the creative mind drives the intellect to sustain life and communicate what we are thinking and feeling. Human mental horsepower comes from our inquisitive, innovative, imaginative, intuitive capacities. We think and act in response to what we need to survive and thrive. We are imagineers and engineers who make an order from chaos by tapping artistic and scientific knowledge. The creative mind ponders abstract overarching ideas with skill and empathy. This transforms humanity by asking better questions and finding the answers that make a better world.

Thinking and reasoning are balanced brain functions. In the creative mind, the right and left brains are perfectly coupled. It is the art-science relationship, beautiful and practical, chaos and order in love. This is the genesis of great theories, works of art, technological breakthroughs, and ideas that enlighten the world. Art and science are states of creative flow. Driven by purpose and passion, they create works of genius and wonder and the exhilaration of discovery. Merged, they are soul mates, mutually enriched and highly creative.

Art is organic, realistic, abstract, visual, musical, narrative, or performative. It is qualitative, inspirational, emotional, and naturally experiential. These are attributes of the right brain. Science is organic, theoretical, biological, medical, social, political, or technical. It is quantitative, logical, rational, and naturally experimental. These are attributes of the left brain. Scientists can be skeptics and artists are often optimists. Both disciplines are deep ways of knowing, observing, and interpreting what is known and unknown. The unique language of art complements science because it explains the unexplainable with empathy and without limitations. Science increases thinking. Art opens feeling. In theory, the artist-scientist individual, or coupling, is the perfect model for the yin-yang of the balanced brain.

We all have the art-science spark. Like Leonardo da Vinci, this light can be brilliant in rare individuals. The German theoretical physicist, Albert Einstein (1879-1955), was an icon of genius whose wizardly ways made him a superstar artist-scientist. He considered the imagination to be more important than knowledge and discovered his 1921 Nobel Prize-winning *Theory of General Relativity* by using creative reasoning and contemplation to prove his famed energy-mass equation, $E = mc^2$. He applied intuitive thought experiments to understand and relate the abstract concepts in his theories. These creative visualizations allowed him to play with his ideas and connect diverse information. Einstein said, "All religions, sciences, and art are branches of the same tree." In a letter to his son, he describes an aspect of creative flow and how the way to learn is by doing something with such enjoyment that time passes without notice. Throughout his lifetime Einstein played the violin and piano avidly. He mused some of his breakthroughs in physics were sparked by the flow of playing music.

Einstein was a lucid dreamer and able to recall vivid details of his dreams. It is storied, as a youth, Einstein had a dream that remained a guiding mental image in scientific adulthood when visualizing his famous theories. In the dream he was sledding down a hill at night under a starry sky. The sled *moved* faster and faster, until it traveled at the speed of light. He looked up, and the heavens were glowing with radiant spectrum colors. Einstein used his curious creative intelligence to compute thoughts and comprehend the mysteries of the cosmos. In later years reflecting on his methodology he said, "I have come to the conclusion that the gift of fantasy has meant more to me than my talent for absorbing knowledge."

In 2016, one hundred years after Albert Einstein's theory of general relativity, science detected the gravitational waves of energy that he predicted, a discovery that will revolutionize the way we look at the Universe. In physics, gravitational waves are ripples in the curvature of spacetime that *move*, traveling outward from the source. Like ripples from the pebble tossed into still water, science is discovering that nature is the model for life and art. The animation of the scientific model for gravitational waves looks like a big spiral of energy as two black holes become one. Chaos becomes a new order. This energy in *motion* creates more energy with a generating and regenerating rhythmic flow. Albert Einstein was an imagineer of this flow, which is now visible and audible because of twenty-first century technology and the imaginative scientists who are discovering how energy *moves* in the cosmos.

Curiosity keeps us wondering and seeking new ways of thinking, doing, and being. It is our inquisitive, playful nature that is eager to learn, experiment, and discover. It makes us fearless and able to bravely know the unknown. An informed sense of purpose, combined with a passionate desire to create something original, fuels innovation. We do what we know. Intellectual prowess expands knowledge. Innovation happens when we synthesize inspiration with our ability to implement an idea. When we tinker, brainstorm, make a sketch, figure things out, and put it all together.

Our daily existence requires creative intelligence, problem-solving, and common sense. Creative chaos to order is part of daily life, whether deciding what to cook for dinner or mapping an urban route with the least traffic. It's a challenge to manage internal thoughts and negotiate external relationships. Critical thinking is how we evaluate, plan, and produce what we need and want. It is a process for self-actualization. We find the value in a problem when we use creative strategies to improve life. We invent simple solutions for the cycling and recycling of ideas and information. Creative problem solving is a way to collaborate and co-create with others through teamwork, sharing ideas and goals, resolving conflicts, and putting forth energy for mutual benefit. This is an important dynamic in interpersonal relationships that relates to our schools, communities, work environments, and local and global leadership. It is essential to the advancement of humanity. The new knowledge economy recognizes that the creativity of individuals and the collective is our most renewable and valuable natural resource.

Learning is the engine of mental creative wellness. It powers the global creative mind. Education is a human right. This lifelong activity engages mental capacities and skill-building, enhances health, and it's great fun! An experiential arts-based education improves verbal, written, math, and science achievement, expands imagination, supports critical thinking, engenders self-discipline and self-awareness, promotes understanding and communication with others, and prepares students with real-life skills. Education systems traditionally model curriculums on STEM (science, technology, engineering, and mathematics), and are expanding toward STEAM by adding "Arts" to the equation. This is a positive shift in the education paradigm. It's important that we value and support the arts and humanities in education and life, for our children and people of all ages and levels of society. Art is not just a subject, it's a way of life. A smart axiom for lifelong creative learning...*no art, no life - know art, know life.*

We all learn differently through various methods. We learn by rote, memorizing and repeating information, or experientially, basically learning by doing. Other types include: kinesthetic - absorbing information by touch, visual - absorbing information by sight, auditory - absorbing information by sound, and olfactory stimulation - absorbing information by smell. Participatory and customized forms of skill-building and learning versus a standardized approach promote creativity and results in better educational outcomes.

A stimulating, self-directed learning experience fosters higher levels of engagement, observation, and competence. Teachers assist in this discovery by providing the tools, models, and skills to apply information. A good teacher knows creativity isn't teachable, and that most education assessments are inadequate for this capacity. They bring the arts into the classroom and lead by example with good creative study habits that instill confidence and the freedom to originate and explore ideas.

The education system is not one size fits all. Homeschooling nurtures a self-directed environment where the teacher designs a curriculum based on the student's skills, interests, and community resources. The boom in online learning gives homeschoolers and students of all ages access to more information and education. Online learning is the new bricks and mortar location for students across the globe. The virtual field of education provides resources and digital curriculums in every area of study. It is impacting cradle to grave learning by making education more accessible, affordable, and relevant to the student. School systems have digital portals for information and remote learning with links to activities and enrichment programs. Education is expanding how we learn and connect in a school community.

Community-based institutions that support adult and continuing education are important resources in the lifelong learning chain. Schools and public libraries provide education and literacy programs for individual and group learning. Libraries are tremendous resources for mental creative wellness. They enrich communities and are an oasis where the creative mind can experience self-directed learning and physically explore books. Books, books, books! Digital and classic bound. May books always be a destination for creative learning. From free access to books and online education, to business resources that support entrepreneurship and retraining, libraries offer learning opportunities for everyone. Children's story hour, visiting authors, lecture series, art exhibits, historical programs, innovative education, maker spaces, senior activities, and diverse community groups - local libraries connect people to each other and a wellspring of literature and information.

Opportunities to learn are abundant with many interesting forms of information and technology available for learners at every level. A fit mind, healthy curiosity, and the discipline to pursue new ideas and seek knowledge are all you need to learn at any age. Memory is the capacity to retain and recall information that is prompted by our sensory perception of sight, sound, touch, smell, or taste. Memories provide a threshold to creativity that activates our cognitive ability to remember what we've learned and experienced. Memory and mental functions are heightened by lifelong creative learning. This stimulates the mind to be at its brainiest and happiest best. Art is smArt. I think and learn, therefore I am creative.

Learning and problem-solving activities offer creative contemplation and entertainment while building mental agility.

Word or number games, puzzles, and mazes are enjoyable ways to test intellectual stamina. We like a mental challenge and the thrill of finding a solution. The brain's natural dopamine release during the experience heightens our sense of reward and expectation. It feels good to win games, solve riddles, make discoveries, innovate, and push mental resolve. The brain likes the smart way to play.

Math is a mighty creative mind sport. There are natural rhythms in mathematic calculations that apply to music and dance. The musical nature of numbers is part of every melody and beat. We count music and counting can be musical. The rhythmic nature of numbers helps measure time and makes us better dancers and toe-tappers. Math dance teaches students experientially by integrating mental and physical elements of learning. Riddles pose abstract questions that require numeric answers. Figuring is fun. "Mathletes" are the young rising stars and arithmetic artists of the modern math world. They represent the new generation of number lovers who will dramatically impact the knowledge economy.

Creative math is a way to go with the flow. There is artistic wisdom in numbers that mirror the life force energy. Sacred geometry in nature defines organic forms that have a sequentially evolving design. The florets in the center of a sunflower, the continuous arching shape of a nautilus shell, a bee's honeycomb, spiraling galaxies in space, and a pebble's effect that *moves* still water are examples of naturally occurring mathematic sequences. This is the numeric architecture of nature. An Italian mathematician named Fibonacci (1175-1250) famously applied this ancient Hindu-Arabic arithmetic concept in his thirteenth century *Book Of Calculation*, the *Liber Abaci*. In the calculation, each number is the sum of the previous two numbers, starting with 0 and 1. The sequence begins 0, 1, 1, 2, 3, 5, 8,

13, 21, 34, 55, 89, 144, 233, 377, 610, 987...and so on, to infinity. It's an elegant mathematical artwork that is seen in nature's beauty and calculated with the creative mind. It represents the divine or golden ratio. The iconic proportions are an underlying design structure in nature that has inspired important works of art and architecture.

Throughout history, the world's greatest creative thinkers have served as ambassadors for art, science, and the humanities. They created social and technological advances that enriched and changed the culture. One such innovator was Benjamin Franklin (1706-1790), a United States Founding Father and statesman distinguished for his diverse talents and accomplishments in the eighteenth century. A true polymath, he was a politician, scientist, inventor, author, and musician. Busy Ben invented bifocals and the lightning rod, and made significant discoveries about electricity and light. He was a prolific communicator who published newspapers, books, and the original *Poor Richard's Almanack*. He established the country's first lending library and post office. Franklin was an artist-scientist and cultural pioneer who used his creative vision to improve society through civic-minded inventiveness, technological advances, printed media, and modern thinking.

Technology has expanded our creative sphere to exciting new dimensions that allows us to share information and experiences in real-time. The entire globe is connected, a very small world after all. The internet has sparked entrepreneurialism and changed the way we learn and express ourselves. We can be informed and communicate in an instant using smart devices and social media. The way we get information is filtered and customized to our interests and beliefs. We choose who and what sources we follow in the media. Ideally, if the corporate culture of digital algorithms doesn't edit choices, we can curate our world view. As connectivity builds a global civilization, we need human gatekeepers to monitor the ethics of what happens with our personal data and the way we get and share information. True creativity needs net neutrality. Being informed about the public path of one's private digital footprint is important. Filtering is an intellectual problem when an artificial influence decides preferences and controls what and how you see on the internet.

With one smartphone the whole world is in your hands, literally. If we want to know or connect to anyone or anything, there's an "app" that applies. We have access to a plethora of television channels, online networks, newspapers, blogs, and platforms for social media that offer hyper-connectivity with anyone we know and don't know. We can post or share any image, meme, opinion, philosophy or manifesto, borrowed or believed. It's a know-on-demand, get-on-demand world and just the beginning of how technology is transforming the human condition. Fallen dictators or natural disasters, the big football championship or wedding celebration, the things you like or don't like, what you ate or where you visited - history is revealed the moment it happens on a hand-held device.

This is giving rise to change and a wellspring of new ideas that are expanding opportunities for shared empathy and expression. It is the new paradigm for creative media in the age of technology. Our technical connections help us communicate, personally and professionally, and open a continual stream of news and sensory information. Technology is the expressway to the global creative mind. It's a powerful co-creator in our daily lives and a medium for individual and collective expression. Connectivity is *mobility*, creativity to go.

With the world in our hands, there's a cautionary tale for those who abuse the realms of technology. The brain-eyes-hands function is a primary facilitator of the creative mind. Humans evolved because we could see and observe the natural world and focus our mind and hands to make and use tools. The tools of technology were invented because of this capacity. Digital technology is linear and one-dimensional. Creativity is nonlinear and multidimensional. Creativity flows when we are connected to sensory awareness and present in the moment of what we can see, hear, touch, smell, and taste.

We risk losing the cerebral mindfulness of natural creative experience when giving too much attention to any technical medium, such as video gaming or compulsive use of social media and texting. This suppresses the ability to perceive sensory things. While walking on the beach, obsessively texting and looking at a device, it's impossible to experience a sentient moment. This can't be good for the brain that is distracted from sensory awareness, or the eyes that are looking at a flat screen and missing the shapes and colors of nature, or the hands which will likely have carpal tunnel syndrome before their time. We are not sentient when looking at a digital device. Here's a metaphor - all the yummy looking food that people post on social media in flat images, you can see it and maybe there's a soundtrack, but you can't touch, smell, or taste it. You can go to a restaurant and savor real food or just look at it on your phone. You can get together with a friend for a warm hug or send a text and get an emoticon.

Face to face versus face to digital, reality versus technology. Though it's vital to modern living and has transformed the global society, technology should never exceed our natural sensory capacities and temporal awareness. It should be a practical balance. There is danger in a digital-only existence and the downgrading of human mental power because of artificial intelligence. Technology and too much screen time can be distracting, addicting, depressing, isolating, and it disrupts sleep. The compulsive habit of needing digital connectivity reduces sensory awareness and our responses to natural experience. It increases stress and the anxiety caused by a fear of missing out. Overdoses are not healthy. In a global culture that promotes hyper-connection while be disconnected, we don't yet have the anthropological data to understand how it may harm our precious eyes, ears, and hands or cause sensory deprivation of the brain.

The internet and our high-tech lifestyles connect and expand the creative mind. These are modern tools for knowing, communicating, and learning. However, the smartest technology is creative thinking, doing, and being. Our brain is the best personal computer. Our eyes and senses are the internet of reality. Our hands facilitate any technology that is needed or desired to create. Technology is a co-creator, however, it doesn't come up with brilliant ideas or make something original. Humans do that.

It's not a coincidence, at Princeton University in the famous physics department where Albert Einstein worked, it is still common practice to use old-fashioned handwriting on chalkboards when scientists are calculating theories. Calculus in *motion* is a beautiful, practical thing. Research shows that college students who take study notes on a computer are less likely to remember and interpret the content than if it were handwritten. Writing by hand, like the process of drawing, stimulates brain development and our ability to learn. These complex tasks involve cognitive, motor, and neuromuscular functions, and require observation with the mind, eyes, and the mind's eye. I tell my students who are looking at their computer to "get ideas" that it's just a tool, and what they originate comes from their mind, not a machine. In the spirit of wellness and common sense, turn the tech OFF. Get a pencil and paper and get your mind *moving* in an organic mental process that is naturally expressive. Set the imagination free. Observe, think, do, and be. Exercise your creative mind.

Mindfulness is a cerebral process inherently linked to creativity. It is a meta-awareness and power of observation we all have. This life-enhancing skill promotes relaxation and homeostasis. The mind is free and the heart is open in real-time. It is a state of attention, not action, a positive intention that is focused on nothing and aware of everything. It is being here now, in the present moment in mind-body-spirit. The one-pointed mind is a pathway to peace and contentment without worry from the past or anxiety about the future. Science recognizes the importance of mindfulness as one of the best ways to reduce stress. The practice of mindful meditation makes new, life-giving connections between brain cells, sparking neurogenesis. Just 10 minutes of practice a day results in improved memory and learning, minimizes stress and pain, and it markedly increases well-being.

We need the stillness of mind to stay *compos mentis*, sane and clear-headed. The mind works hard to keep the body going, so it's important to take care of it. This requires unplugging from technology, finding a quiet oasis, and giving only the moment your attention. Mindfulness is a way to relax that requires slowing down and taking time to be in time. Empty the mind to become full. Less thinking, more feeling. Less worry, more trust. Less stress, more energy. Less distraction, more connection. Less attachment, more abundance. The pathway to positive evolution is through involution, the inward curve toward the center of one's self.

Creative mindfulness is a practice when we are present doing *creativity* and not other things, like multitasking. We all do it. We perform many daily tasks simultaneously, rarely for better and mostly for worse. Neuroscience shows how the brain loves to do one thing and is brilliantly efficient without diversion. We may feel good because there's a sense of accomplishment when doing two or more things at once. Still, asking the brain to multitask requires an enormous amount of energy to function in many directions. The mind in a singular mode can be a peak creative experience, in the flow with what we know and open to new knowing without distraction.

Throughout the day, consciously and unconsciously, the creative mind is working 24/7. Even in the restful realm of sleep, it is analyzing, reviewing, and organizing daily mental data. While asleep, the brain works like a supercomputer to process sensory input with dreaming being the output. We dream to remember and forget, to heal and restore. We intuit abstract concepts, solve problems, and seem to achieve what eludes us in wakefulness. Dreaming is a mental and physical process, as well as a language. If you've ever fallen into a deep sleep and awakened with fresh insight, you know its healing effects. We spend nearly a third of our lives asleep. At every age, it's essential to get enough sleep for optimal mental functioning. A tired brain is stressed, moody, impatient, and lacks focus. A rested brain is less stressed, composed, creative, and focused. When we are learning, it requires long periods of restfulness to have time to process new information and knowledge. Sleep relates to natural circadian rhythms and how we respond to light in an environment. Balanced sleeping supports optimal health.

The healthier we sleep, the more we dream. I'm a lucid dreamer, and when engaged in learning or artistic endeavoring, my dreams are often a continuation of the ideas or emotions occupying me. These brightly colored dreams offer symbolic insights and provide a narrative I apply to my conscious thinking. In childhood, we naturally have a gift of fantasy for dreaming about what we imagine and may become in our lives, and this can continue in adulthood. The mind at rest is a creative wonderland. It's usually good advice to sleep on it. Give your mind a rest because wisdom is often revealed in the cinema of the night. Sweet, smart dreams.

What is your mental creative wellness?

8: Physical Creative Wellness

creative doing, physical *movement*, sensory response,
expression **art**iculated, self-care, play, sex, home chores,
fitness, sports, human-powered activities, rhythm, dance,
making music, mind-body-spirit exercise, what *moves* you

Creativity is physical. It's a natural *movement* that **artic**-ulates expression. We experience creativity with the body, whether art-making, art-taking, or art-giving. The process acti-vates sensory responses and primal rhythms. Physical creative wellness is feeling and *moving* with the flow. The italicized *lo-comotion* words in this narrative emphasize the importance of the corporeal nature of creativity. It requires the body to be present in the moment, in mind and spirit. This means showing up for practice, doing creativity, and *leaning* into it with intention. The creative flow isn't stagnant, it *moves* and changes. In metaphor, even the still water is *moving* and alive before the pebble reorganizes the space. This transforms energy, the physics of the physical, and creativity is in *motion*.

We are physical organisms built to survive and thrive in our environment. The human body is a well-designed structure for creating life. It is a series of interdependent systems that keep us lively and growing. These include skeletal, muscular, nervous, endocrine, cardiovascular, lymphatic, respiratory, di-gestive, urinary, and reproductive systems. On the outside, the limbs and facial features are symmetrical. On the inside, the brain and organs are asymmetrical. The body is a miracle of nature. It is a microcosm of the macrocosm and an archetype for the physical mechanisms of the cosmos. Like the animated figure *Creative Being*, the human form stands balanced on the physical Earth. Our natural architecture is living matter enlivened by breath. It reflects the subtle body, a sacred form of physical being known in Tibetan Buddhism as the rainbow body. Balanced and whole, the sentient creative body is a somatic element of the luminous physical Universe with its colorful diversity in *motion*. Creativity is a pure vitality we know and feel. Knitting or bungee jumping, it's active.

Body-on creative experience stimulates the senses and heightens perception. It activates the benefits of the brain-eyes-hands function. We think about, see, and do creativity. It is the palpable response to our thoughts and feelings. The creative body *motivates* the creative mind and releases endorphins with positive effects, prompting neurogenesis in the brain. A physical creative wellness routine combined with proper nutrition and adequate fluids supports optimal performance and health. We all need physical fitness and *movement*, about 30 minutes every day with additional moderate to vigorous aerobic activity based on interest, ability, and overall health. *Move* it or lose it. Some people are more active because they are athletic and dedicate extra time to exercise. Most lifestyles can include some form of physical exercise that is a way to express the body in *motion*. Creative exertion is a good thing. It restores stamina essential to health and longevity. A physically active and creative lifestyle boosts the immune system, reduces stress, enhances self-esteem, maintains muscles and bones, controls weight and blood pressure, and improves sleep. The body reminds us that self-care is the way to stay healthy.

A physical practice is a portal for connecting with the life force energy and creating health. Over millennia, a global culture of exercise systems have evolved with disciplines rooted in ancient traditions and belief. Yoga, Tai Chi, and QiGong are mind-body-spirit practices that feature a series of *movements* that are not just artistic-looking calisthenics. These life skills are cultivated over time to *move* vital energy within the body toward the right relationship to health and well-being. Mind-body exercise connects the practitioner with spirit. It is an art form involving gestures and postures that relax and strengthen the body with the intention of creating balance. Mind-body interventions and exercises benefit the nervous, endocrine, and immune systems, and are common complementary health approaches. An ongoing personal practice keeps the body fit and flexible, builds core strength, and regulates breathing and circulation.

Breath is an essential element of mind-body exercise that raises self-awareness and reduces stress. Techniques to control breath allow for the deep breathing needed to pause and center energy. It is a powerful way to connect the mind and body with spirit. It is instinctively part of any physical practice or sport. We breathe to support the activities we are doing. When we are *moving* and doing creativity in the flow, our breathing flows naturally. The process promotes homeostasis. The physical body operates at various speeds, fast or slow, and respiration and oxygenation respond. In exercise and sports, mindfulness connects breath to support performance.

My favorite physical creative practice is the mindfulness of open water swimming in a lake or ocean. Breathing is essential to the ritual of diving into the water. That initial buoyant air in my lungs prepares me for the temperature, which can be chilly where I swim in Maine. *Moving* through the water, I breathe to support exertion. I often float, balancing my body on the surface of the water. Depending on the wind, my oxygenated lungs and core strength keep me afloat. I can feel the weightless flow of my body of water in a geographic body of water. It is a profound way to open sensory awareness and connect with the *movement* of the Earth.

Touching our physical body to the physical Earth grounds energy and nurtures the soul. Some of my most bright ideas and healing insights have come to me while swimming or walking. In my experience, walking time is often creative thinking time and a way to exhale the day. Finding a physical place to let the mind wander releases negative energy and thoughts while building the body's natural strength and confidence. I like to walk down the beach at a good pace while pondering a question. Then, as I walk back along my trail of footprints, the answer is often clear. Mindful walking meditation happens in any environment where you are physically grounded. Walking in an urban environment provides both physical and cultural exhilaration with varied rhythms and sensory stimulation. Wherever you are, go for a walk and leave your creative footprints.

Sports are a form of creative play. Playing a sport directs the body's athletic skill to focus on physical performance. It requires channeling mental and spiritual powers to excel. Structured or team-based sports help participants learn respect for rules and guidelines while building goal-oriented values and a sense of competition. Playing a team sport taps creative thinking and problem-solving in the huddle and on the field. It gives players the ability to implement winning strategies and outplay the opponent. The whole sports culture is creative. Competitive sports teams and athletes have colorful, high-performance uniforms and equipment that are high-tech and high-fashion. There is artistic embellishment on skis, skates, snowboards and surfboards, and all forms of athletic gear. The bright colors, energized graphics, branded products, and enhanced media associated with sports inspire excitement and generate a strong identity for teams and fans. Beyond design elements, the way an athlete performs is a physical and visual form of art. The performance draws us creatively to sports when watching a figure skater land a triple axel, a runner's rhythmic strides, or a quarterback make the winning touchdown pass. Athletic physicality is like poetry in *motion*.

Human-powered activity can be a peak creative experience fueled only by the energy that our body makes naturally. Aerobic exercise, walking, hiking, running, swimming, surfing, tennis, golf, kayaking, cycling, skiing, skating, snowboarding, mountain climbing, scuba diving, court and field sports. These activities require physical strength, skill, and *movement*. A sport that generates human horsepower is good exercise and generally provides a sense of well-being and accomplishment. It is something we look forward to that defines our physical personality and interests. When the amazing human body is the vehicle, the mind and spirit enjoy the ride. The creative body likes to express itself in a physical place or space. Nature is a big outdoor playground. We also get physical at the gym, dance studio, or in a workout space at home.

Play is the workhorse of the creative body. Playtime is learning time and an opportunity to engage in an uninhibited activity that prompts whimsical thinking and doing. It is an improvisational act that drives innovation and self-discovery. It is fun, rules or no rules. When we play, we recreate. Recreational activity is something we enjoy that is rejuvenating. Even common things that we don't enjoy, like household chores or yard work, can be creative play. I admit, I like the sport of dance vacuuming. We can glean insights of beauty while raking leaves or walking the dog. Practicing creative playfulness as we *move* things around is a way to improve our physical health and space, and keep the puppy happy.

Our corporeal nature loves to play. It is a primal desire that excites expression and arouses the senses. Sex can be a very playful and sensual physical activity. Emotional and physical romance is how we creatively attract partners and show affection, and it keeps the relationship interesting over time. An act of physical love and union can create the ultimate human creation, a human baby. Coitus and the birthing process invoke life-giving rhythms and *movement* while heightening body awareness. We draw on our physical capacity to use breath as we in-spire, breathing in, then out, letting energy flow. Sexual orgasm is a peak creative experience. Playful ecstatic release is how it physically feels, a systemic rush that uplifts energy and expands bliss. It is an intimate physical sensation when the life force energy is *moving* in the body with full flow and pleasure.

Vibrationally, we are plugged in, the body is electric. If the human form is an example of the energy dynamics in the Universe, then the cosmos must be made up of color, light, music, and dance. All that energy in *motion* needs a little dance party atmosphere with infinite gleaming stars and rotating matter pulsing to the beat. The primal way we relate to music and dance allows us to release and rejuvenate at any tempo from classical to hard rock. The performing arts encompass elements of breath, rhythm, and *movement* in the physical act of expression. Music, dance, drama, improvisation, and visual arts activate physical experience, whether you are the artist or audience. These are common forms of the creative body expressed.

The vibrational quality of music has physical effects on the maker and listener. Music is something we hear and feel all over the body. It is this *movement* that transforms and heals. Musical rhythm vibrationally activates auditory and motor systems in trained and spontaneous ways. Playing a musical instrument is a physical experience that requires motor skills, rhythmic awareness, and the ability to listen and remember notes and sequences. The act of playing an instrument is known to have both calming and rousing physical effects. It doesn't mean that just quiet music is calming or loud music is rousing. You can feel relaxed when hard rocking the guitar with the amps turned up, just be mindful of your precious hearing. Electronic, percussion, wind, string, or keyboard - playing an instrument requires the body and creative muse to be in sync.

A master musician's performance can be a wonder of physicality. It takes core strength and stamina to play a musical instrument. Rockers with beefcake physiques don't just go to the gym. Playing a gig can be a workout. I'm a classical music fan, and it amazes me to see the physicality required to play an instrument. A gifted musician embodies the instrument with vitality and emotion. It is this physicality that makes *moving* music. I would love to have witnessed the great Hungarian pianist and composer Franz Liszt (1811-1886) playing the piano. Franz was a brain-eyes-hands virtuoso whose advanced technical skill and luminous interpretations on the piano made him a legendary performer. He had a bold physical presence and was famous for his force of precision and singular style that would leave audiences memorized. When he played the piano, it was as if he had three hands. Dramatically complex, playing Liszt's compositions requires herculean musical skill and physical dexterity. Hearing and seeing a performance of the energized piano solo in his symphonic work, *Totentanz* is a marvel of artistry and athleticism.

Performing music brings people physically together in a group, band, or orchestra. It nurtures communal rhythm and vibration. A drumming circle connects the participating drummers in a democratic way with all who physically join the beat considered equal in their musical contribution. It's an exhilarating form of group-conscious music making that aligns physical elements with spiritual practice. Singing is the creative body in harmony with the creative voice. The physical act of singing relieves stress, helps balance heart rate, and improves breathing. It exercises the lungs and builds core strength. Singing is a way to express emotions and tell stories. When we sing or play music with a group, our physical awareness and connection to others is heightened. Physically performing and sharing music is a peak creative experience.

When music and dance combine, the body's auditory and motor systems merge, crystalizing rhythm and *motion* in an experiential process. Dance exalts the creative body. People love to dance. Ballroom, country, line, ballet, modern, hip-hop, disco, belly, boogie, tap, salsa, folk, swing, slow, trance, tango, waltz, vogue, or any other *move* you can maneuver. The body feels the vibes and articulates new forms and gestures. We identify with cultural beats and rhythms that bring people together in harmony and give us a sense of belonging to the tribe. Dance is often part of community ritual and celebration. It helps us connect with others and understand the rhythms of physical relationships within a population. We find our groove and tap into the beat of humanity. Dance is a healthy exercise that supports balance, strength, coordination, and range of *motion*. Like aerobic exercise, the activity enhances mood and well-being and is one of the most enjoyable ways to shake it all out and express physicality.

Visual art making is a technical and physical activity that requires dexterity and observational skills. Just as a musician embodies the instrument, the visual artist embodies the medium. Drawing activates body energy. It can feel physically satisfying to create an expressive work with strong contour lines and rich values. I have observed artists drawing when their body gestures imitate the subject of the work. Like the ability to draw, it takes brain-eyes-hands skill to paint at any level of ability. From finger paint to refined brushstrokes, the fluidity of painting allows the artist to *move* and flow with the medium. Sculpting or building a three-dimensional work of visual art requires the body to facilitate a physical form. Whether carving a piece of sculpture from stone or throwing a clay pot on a wheel, giving art a physical form requires the body to be strong, agile, focused, and balanced. An artistic medium that gets the body physically active outdoors, such as photography or plein air painting, is a way to explore the art of nature. In any medium, hands-on, body-on creativity **art**iculates expression.

Creativity is physical. Taking care of the body that makes it happen, matters. The quality and quantity of our daily food and exercise fuels the body. Healthy habits create health. Maintaining good nutrition and a proactive wellness routine builds the immune system and keeps the body strong and fit. It is also important to rest the body. Creative exertion aids sleep and releases tensions. The better we sleep, eat, and exert energy, the more we can perform at an optimal level.

However you practice, play, sport, exercise, occupy, propel, manifest, rest, or *move*, it can be an opportunity to create wellness. The creative body is active - doing, making, forming, exercising, playing, going, shifting, and changing. The creative body is present - thinking, observing, practicing, focusing, feeling, enjoying, and being. The well-designed human physique is an exquisite work of art.

What is your physical creative wellness?

9: Spiritual Creative Wellness

creative being, Creator-creature connection, prayer, spirituality,
hope factor, religious groups and services, sacred symbols,
illumination arts, sentient nature, holy ground, meditation,
ritual, peak creative experience, emotions in *motion*, love

Creativity is spiritual. The sacred life is illuminated by our inner light and a deep yearning for good. Spiritual creativity is the realm of love, joy, gratitude, compassion, empathy, and hope. Inspired and in spirit, we aspire to be happy and healthy and to create our best lives. Spiritual creative wellness happens in moments of grace when we are aligned with the Creator and Universe. It completes the mind-body-spirit trinity that makes the creative wheel of life turn with loving evolution. Mental and physical capacities facilitate creative expression. Spirituality seeds purpose and sparks passion. The creative spirit leads us on the pathway to divinity and holy ground.

The Creator-creature connection is profound and personal. Spirituality is rooted in what we value and believe. Seeking is inherent to spirituality. It is the soul's journey guided by higher consciousness and a higher power. We are seekers looking for true knowledge as we light the inner lamp. We seek meaning in human existence and faith in a divine source. A spiritual seeker may worship in their community, travel to a destination of devotion, build an altar in a personal space, or find sanctuary in nature. They investigate the mysteries of the spirit through sacred ritual and meditation. Seekers find faith within. There is inner guidance and enlightenment in the intimate dialogue we share with Creator. It is an eternal conversation, informed by love, when we speak with creative true voice and listen with the heart.

There is beneficial biology related to belief and spiritual practice. Science suggests practicing faith enhances health and well-being similar to the benefits of creativity. The key is focusing on positive outcomes and *moving* with intention towards what we need, want, and believe. Having confidence in our resilience and highest potential is a way to create a good life. It is the hope factor. Positive psychology heals the mind-body-spirit. It revitalizes and improves our life condition. The placebo effect of positive belief is activated by our sentient nature. It opens spiritual awareness and the healing powers of love. We can create what we believe. The key is remaining true to beliefs and optimistic about the future.

Prayer and meditation engender mental and physical healing. The medical and pastoral intersects as we hope for health and happiness. In medicine, this is what is intended through intercessory prayer when the act of praying for others is a healing tool of faith. Sometimes, suffering brings us to our spirituality, because we are caring for a loved one or seeking a way to care for ourselves. Studies show that prayer and meditation affect the brain in ways that reduce emotional and physical stress and boost the immune system. These benefits occur, in part, because of the essential nature of spiritual practice and one's strength of belief. Prayer is the practice of positive affirmation and devotion. However practiced, prayer is a conscious creative connection to the spirit. The flow of creativity, as a sacred act, is like praying.

Spirituality is a measure of what we value and love most. Creativity connects us to spirit through our emotions and actions. It is the inspired realm of peak creative experience. These are life's finest moments when we are engaged and in spirit, *moving* with the flow of expression, creating what we believe. It can be something we make or do, a loved creative thing. It gives agency and spiritual ownership that speaks to who we are and what we believe. It's a natural high and state of awe when we are open to magic and achieving our highest, happiest potential. A peak creative experience heightens the senses and awakens the spirit. It is the blissful response to a creative event - the summer vacation moment when you launch the kayak on a still lake, an evening out in the big city with a loved friend, or taking a pottery class and seeing your first glazed pot coming out of the kiln. It is something we look forward to and keep in memory as a powerfully poignant symbol of joy. The experience has a shining quality that resonates in the soul. We feel excitement and contentment and are free to be ourselves at our best. Like an epiphany it is the sweet spot that brings us into the right relationship with the moment and life force energy. The rapture of the adventure is transformative and life-changing. Peak creative experiences articulate our purpose, passion, and divinity.

The arts are fundamental to how we know and practice religion. Spirituality is sanctified through prayer, chant, ritual, meditation, and storytelling. It is expressed with music, dance, visual art, and liturgy. The aesthetics of belief are rich with artistic symbols, ambient sounds, and narrative language. Individually and collectively, the arts illuminate the story of faith and how we express spirituality. Expressing the creative spirit happens in beautiful and familiar ways. Every religion has an aesthetic style that varies according to faith and local traditions. The Christian culture is beautifully diverse, from the practical and minimalistic lifestyle of the Shakers to the grand pageantry of the Catholic Church. Religious art creates a sacred record and environment for devotees. Holy texts, art, music, traditional costumes, ceremonial objects, and the purifying sensation of incense are artistic elements that infuse and enrich spiritual practice and celebration. A religious community supports creative culture. Sharing an art experience and worshiping with the fellowship of believers uplifts the spirit and heightens creativity. We come together on holy ground. These are meaningful moments when we are kindred with something pure, powerful, and immensely wonderful.

Art is the foundation of sacred architecture and design. Throughout history, monumental works have existed in cultures around the world. Past and present, these landmarks represent masterful art, design, and engineering. Christianity, Islam, Judaism, Hinduism, Buddhism, and many earth-based religions have artistic traditions, both in practice and the places where worshipers gather. Religious institutions are often cultural benefactors that provide a community venue for the arts.

An example is *La Sagrada Família Cathedral* in Barcelona, the great unfinished masterpiece by the Spanish Catalan architect, Antoni Gaudi (1852-1926). A pioneer of the *Modernista* movement, Gaudi created awe-inspiring whimsical architecture influenced by Gothic, Islamic, and Art Nouveau styles. Formed by nature's geometry, his buildings look like nothing else ever built. *La Sagrada* features colorful mosaics and organic spaces and spires shaped and curved as if ocean waves flowed through them. The structure has massive catenary arches, and dramatic pillars that are like a forest reaching to the heavens. Remarkably, the Cathedral is still under construction today honoring Gaudi's original plans and vision. It is a popular cultural destination for tourists and spiritual seekers.

Music is omnipresent in sacred tradition. Song or chant, choral or instrumental, music expresses the soul and is the sound of faith. Sacred music reflects a devotion to God with holy rhythm and melody. Great composers and musicians, inspired by spiritual belief, created some of the world's most loved musical works that define cultural and religious traditions. Music inspired by faith and spiritual connection creates a transcendent experience for the music maker and listener. Our innate musical spirituality is why experiencing it can be so *moving* and joyful. Music is a sensory medium that speaks to universal truth and what matters most. It invokes our greatest strength, the power of belief.

Sacred hymns or anthems are profoundly *moving* when musical memories are recalled. The sounds and sound memories of certain types of instruments seem to invoke spiritualism with their tone and vibration. The bell, drum, flute, guitar, piano, organ, harp, and zither create the diverse and familiar sounds of faith-inspired music. The pipe organ is an instrument that taps my musical memory of faith. The sound is reminiscent of primordial bellowing and heavenly piping. It's a grand instrument in size and scale that has a cosmic presence when played in an acoustic theatre. The big airy tones and intense acoustic range are a pure vibration akin to the breath and rhythm of life, what glorification and eternity must sound like.

The instrument of the human voice is an essential component of spiritual practice. Through music and narrative, the vibration of chant, prayer, song, and spoken word expresses the creative spirit. These mediums are both deeply personal and expansively inclusive. The human voice preaches faith and encompasses the ideals of an individual or group of followers. The liturgy of spiritual practice is richly endowed with expressive invocation that requires the singer, sayer, prayer, and listener to engage with divine intention. The sounds of reading or reciting sacred scripture affirms the seeker's faith and creates an audio memory of the word of God. Sacred songs and texts reflect the histories and mysteries of belief. Religious narratives include literary oracles in every language that document faith and respond to a basic human need to make sense of living. Some of the most informative and wondrous artifacts are hand-written and illuminated manuscripts from cultures around the globe. Those created during the Middle Ages were religious or historic annuals. Some of the rare codices and sacred scrolls that have survived are brilliantly colored with finely detailed il-lustrations depicting spiritual text and imagery. Manuscripts were created on parchment or vellum and skillfully embellished with pure gold or silver leaf, thus making this unique form of book art an illumination of illumination.

Visual art in spiritual practice gives the seeker a picture of faith. It prompts mental imagery to visualize the elements of a belief system. Churches, mosques, temples, synagogues, and prehistoric caves are adorned with sacred images. The art of devotion is illuminated in paintings, frescos, sculptures, and ar-chitectural details. The lexicon of sacred imagery includes sym-bols, icons, and figurative representations of worship. Sacred artworks decorate faith-based institutions or a personal space. Spiritual seekers display artful objects of devotion and medita-tion in a home altar or sanctuary. Personal altars can be created in a favorite room, garden spot, daily journal, or workspace. Our most vivid and visual form of divinity is the intimate, inner view in the mind's eye during prayer and meditation. Sacred images are seen and felt, even when the eyes are closed.

Visual symbolism appears in many genres of sacred art. It informs and speaks to the spiritual collective conscious and unconscious. Some symbols share universal interpretations. A bird in flight represents the free and transcendent spirit. A tree with expanding branches and roots illustrates connectedness of the Earth and Universe. A triangle pointing upward is the ascent to Heaven. A cross shows the cardinal points in space in divine union. Stars symbolize light and a higher order. A spiral is a circle set free and an iconic image of the life force energy in *motion*. It is the animated change of order to chaos and the generative and regenerative cycles of birth, life, death, and rebirth.

Seen in the composition of paintings, the shapes of rooms and windows, and meditative designs, the circle is a distinctive geometric symbol represented in sacred art. With no beginning or end, circles represent eternity and the wholeness of life. Though geometric, it is a perfect organic form that mirrors nature and reflects the interconnectedness of all life. The shape is integral to forms of spiritual practice as a unifying symbol that invokes healing and completeness. Hindu and Buddhist traditions have highly artistic and colorful mandalas with a central round design, sometimes intersected by a square. A circle reflects spiritual synthesis and connection to Heaven. It is the opposite of a square, which represents physical matter and connection to Earth. Regardless of proportion, when integrated, they have unified strength and spatial beauty. Throughout history, the geometric form inspired and informed works by artists and architects using the divine ratio and naturally aesthetic designs that represent spiritual harmony and balance. Like the image of *Creative Being*, we are aligned, connected with nature and the Creator. It is all interconnected, indeed.

The creative spirit is part of nature, not apart. In the right relationship to Earth, we recognize that human existence is possible because of the bounty of the natural environment. We must creatively and sustainably live on our mothership Earth and have respect for all the gifts of life. Within the natural world, we find sacred sanctuaries that connect us to essence on holy ground. Nature exalts cerebral awareness and reminds us that we are keepers of Earth as we endeavor to conserve natural resources while flourishing. Our dear planet benefits from the creative world citizen who is spiritually and environmentally aware. We are responsible for Earth's wellness. Each of us must value and venerate all that it generates and regenerates. Our senses need the natural environment to retreat for spiritual self-care, to cleanse the toxins and sins of modern living. Nature is like a big outdoor church, a cathedral of the sky and land, abundant with precious life-giving water, air, soil, and the biological diversity that makes life possible. We are not separate from Earth, we come from the same organic stuff and are interconnected.

The cycles of nature throughout the year are times when we recognize and celebrate spiritual traditions in relationship to Earth. The spring and autumn equinoxes, summer and winter solstices, cross-quarter days, and astronomical calendars inspire creativity. Cultural traditions evolved around agricultural and spiritual seasons that honor the natural environment. What we sow, nurture, harvest, and celebrate keeps our creative spirit strong throughout the year. Spiritual holidays, festivals, and celebrations bring people together in solidarity at gatherings that give meaning to life. Common ground for the common good. These are joyful times of fasting and feasting, costumes and decorations, humor and cheer, music-making, singing, and dancing. Tidings and traditions of sacred living are special moments when we shine a light on our inner light and share the light with others.

Gratitude and reverence are peak creative experiences. Sanctified through the lens of creativity, we show devotion and love to our kindred and the divine. Times of spiritual right relationship are creative opportunities to express feelings for loved ones, friends, neighbors, and all people. A thoughtful deed, a simple act of kindness, an acknowledgment of affection - these are our truest expressions. Handwritten notes, heartfelt gifts, goodwill gestures, and prayers of hope are expressive mediums for showing and sharing our faith in those we love. With emotions in *motion,* life and love are celebrated.

Spiritual creative wellness informs and transforms the very personal experience of faith. The mind and body cannot be strong without the spirit. We must practice creativity of the soul as part of a proactive wellness routine. Spiritual creativity is *sine qua non.* It is essential. Creativity exists because we are spiritual beings who have love and reverence for life. Love and creativity are sacred experiences that inspire personal epiphanies. An epiphany is a rare and enlightening moment that awakens a new awareness. It gives hope and a better understanding of our relationship to everything. The sentient state *moves* us to make brilliant creative breakthroughs and be our best and brightest. A religious epiphany is when a spiritual seeker aligns with the sacred source of faith. It's an affirmation of a belief that enlightens the path and directs our moral compass. Like a star in darkness guiding the way, an epiphany is an empowered state of awareness that connects our essence to the Divine.

The lush nature of the soul is revealed through conscious creative experience. With hope and faith, we walk into the light and the creative spirit takes flight. On the creative journey, spirituality is in every direction. Divinity happens in the simple and remarkable moments of daily living. I wish you peace and *Namaste*, the Spirit in me honors the Spirit in you.

What is your spiritual creative wellness?

10: Environment Creative Wellness

Earth consciousness, environmental stewardship, habitat,
being in nature, having a vista, color, light, circadian rhythms,
seasons and cycles, atmospheric activities, everyday environs,
personal space, creative ecosystems, travel, special places

The environment is creative. It is where we are and what surrounds us. We are always in an environment, the scene where life happens. The way we experience it is a creative opportunity that requires being extant, present in a place. We live in social, cultural, and natural habitats. We create in our home, work, community, and in nature. All human habitat is creative. Circumstances and conditions impact our surroundings and we adapt to fit. Environment creative wellness is the habitat where we survive and thrive.

The Earth is our natural environment. Gaia, the Great Earth Mother, is an ancient Greek goddess whose namesake principle suggests all life is interconnected on the planet in a shared and complex ecosystem. It sustains millions of plant and animal species, different types of organisms, and nearly 8 billion humans. From the tiniest nanobe to the largest tree, from the butterfly to you and me, Earth is in a creative bio-dance with an endless exchange of biodynamic energy. We are part of nature, not apart. This relationship is primordial. We cannot be separate because we are biologically connected and exist in it. The air we breathe and ground beneath our feet, we are living on this amazing planet and it lives in us. We are Mother Nature's children. The rhythms of nature are in human DNA, whether residing in an urban, suburban, or rural setting. Wherever the environment, the body instinctively responds to planetary cycles and seasons. Being in nature awakens our senses and sustains physical existence. Elements of the natural environment - the fertile earth, fresh air, fiery sun, and flowing water - Earth gives her creative gifts so we can live.

Environmental stewardship reminds us to consider the biological, geological, and ecological history of the planet and how we abuse or respectfully use limited natural resources. We are co-creators with Earth. The negative effects of climate change, or one devastating earthquake, volcanic eruption, or meteorite and humans would be great, like the dinosaurs. Our great civilization may become extinct. The global environment affects us all. Collectively, human creativity must be applied to new energy technologies, environmental education, and living sustainably. Recycling isn't enough. We must become creative consumers; and learn to buy, and use what we buy, more consciously. We can creatively solve the climate change problem by innovating and improving how we live. Everyone is responsible for protecting the Earth's beauty and abundance for future generations. It is essential to value and conserve precious natural resources. Remember - nothing wasted, everything gained. Recycling and renewing what we need, speaks to the spirit of innovation that evolved our species. Planetary homeostasis is the way to human homeostasis. It is all connected.

The heart of **Eart**h is art. We experience natural elements with the senses. To see a blue sky, hear a songbird's symphony, feel the warmth of sunshine, smell a balsam forest, or taste a freshly picked fruit - these are sensory moments in the natural world. The senses imprint natural experience in the psyche and are a measure of our health-happiness. With our eyes and mind's eye, we all need a vista of nature. It is a special place on Earth we know and remember that resonates with our soul. A loved vista strengthens and grounds our connection to the living Earth. We feel this aliveness. It's a scene that draws us away to a familiar horizon beyond the vanishing point. From this perspective, we can reflect on the past and present with hope for the future. A vista of nature is a view or memory of a view that recalls the sensory beauty and expansiveness of an environment. The city dweller may have a vista that includes an architectural landscape or open space with the sky's natural light. A suburbanite's vista may be tree-lined streets with manicured green lawns and colorful gardens. Country folks have many vistas of rural land with mountains and bodies of water.

Research shows that having a window view with a pleasant landscape increases productivity in the workplace, enhances learning in classrooms, and supports recovery in hospitals. There is psychological evidence that people who live in proximity to natural locations and green spaces, whether a rural forest or city park, enjoy increased physical vitality and longevity. The human brain is happier and healthier when in nature. It activates sensory awareness and creativity in ways that reduce stress and promote mindfulness. Physically and emotionally, we respond to the colors, light, organic textures, smells, and sounds. This is environment creative wellness.

Sensory awareness in nature renews our connectedness to Earth. We need to experience the natural world as part of a proactive wellness routine. It is the way to connect with our sentient nature. Feeling the earth beneath our feet is a direct dose of grounding energy. Natural experiences inspire creativity, whether in nature or an ambient environment. It's vital to have natural, undistracted time that allows for organic responses in balance with the artificial stimulation of technology. A television or the smartest device can't imitate the sight, sound, feel, smell, or salty taste of an ocean breeze. Less screen time, more scene time. Less digital algorithm, more natural rhythm.

Turning tech OFF turns sensory awareness and the creative flow ON.

Take time to look at a tree. With more than 60,000 species on the planet, we are fortunate to share our environment with trees of all shapes and sizes. Trees inspire our creative nature and teach us about human nature. These woody perennials enrich our lives and can feel familiar, like an old friend. Landmarks of our natural experience, trees are among the oldest, continuously living organisms, with some species thriving for thousands of years. Longevity is the way of the tree in an environment where it can flourish away from the buzz-saw sound of change. Trees mark a sense of time in a place. We plant them to celebrate traditions, create a landscape, or honor people. We need trees and forests to produce life-giving oxygen and remove the carbon dioxide in the atmosphere. There is a spiritual connection to trees. Rooted in our habitats and histories, we grow and expand together through the seasons. Like a cathedral, the tree reaches up towards the light and Heaven while its roots reach down into the rich Earth in equal balance. It is the symbol of the Tree of Life, a universal metaphor for the harmony between heavenly and earthly forces. It resembles our animated figure in this story, *Creative Being*. One can imagine the *motion*, like a tree's branches with the leaves swaying in the wind, grounded and growing with the life force energy.

The natural world and our everyday environs influence sensory stimuli. The quality of sound and air, spatial dynamics, and the safety and comfort we feel in an environment activates creative flow. Habitat impacts how and what we create. Natural light and the full spectrum of colors it engenders increases creativity and well-being. Light affects how we experience any environment. Artificial or natural, the lamp by the bed or the sunlight coming through a window, light makes color visible.

The body's inborn circadian rhythms respond to light. It prompts us to be active when the days are long and rest when the days are short. The cycles of creativity are part of our environmental body clock and the daily patterns of day and night. Light energizes health and vitality. Our eyes speak to the brain, and we evolve as nocturnal or diurnal creatures. Biologically, humans need the light of activity and the darkness of rest for optimal wellness. During winter, when there is less daylight, we tend to act like hibernating bears. We sleep more, are less active, and get a little chubby. Like nutrition, it is important to attune to the quality and quantity of light in our environment. Seasonal Affective Disorder, or SAD, is a depressive mood condition caused by a lack of natural light. The imbalance is helped with vitamin supplements and by creating a lighted environment for therapeutic effect. A healthy dose of ambient lighting feels good because the body absorbs the organic nutrients natural light radiates.

Color creates an atmosphere that calms or rouses the senses. The quality and quantity of colors in our daily lives influences how we feel in any environment. Colors can have a universal effect. Red feels warm and active. Violet feels cool and meditative. Green is considered to be the most balancing and healing color. Psychological studies show the color green reduces stress, improves concentration, inspires creativity, and boosts *motivation*. As the painter's eye knows, seeing color is unique to the individual. In any environment, there is a need and preference for colors that vibrate harmoniously with our personal spectrum. We each have a rainbow code. These are the colors that affect who we are and how we survive and thrive. Creating spaces and enjoying places with ambient colors and light increases wellness. The symbiotic relationship we have to color in an environment includes where we are, what we do, the food we eat, the clothes we wear, our home and possessions. Color is light and not limited to an external environment. It permeates and nourishes our bodies and lifestyles in sensory ways.

Color and light are part of the show when we observe nature's creativity. Sky gazers look for star clusters, orbiting planets, and celestial phenomenon with eye and telescope. The sky can be full of radiant colors and cloud sculptures in the forms of cumulus, nimbus, stratus, and cirrus. The crazy, ever-changing weather requires us to adapt to any natural environment. From a fog's gentle kiss to a face slap by the polar vortex, a weather phenomenon makes for some very creative observation and participation. It also requires us to be practical and prepared - to batten down the hatches and ride out storms or wear flip-flops and slather on the sunscreen. Chasing eclipses or rainbows, and tornadoes with appropriate caution, can be a peak creative experience. These phenomena are documented by some of the most remarkable photographs taken in this century. Looking and listening, the sky offers atmospheric activities and creative observation throughout the seasons.

Human habitats must be shared with natural habitats. The creative naturalist is a keeper and knower of the way to live in balance with ecology. Ecosystems sustain biodiversity and biodiversity sustains ecosystems, nature's creative yin-yang. Observing plants and animals in the wild is a way to know the natural world and wonders of discovery. Fishing, kayaking, boating, paddle boarding, surfing, swimming, hiking, and walking are outdoor activities with a natural point of view. Backpacking on conservation trails or visiting a park are creative opportunities for the amateur biologist with a pair of binoculars who ventures to the estuary, wetland, woodland, grassland, or desert habitat.

Birds exist in nearly every habitat on the globe. Birding can be a passionate creative hobby and an interesting way to learn how a natural habitat maintains a species. From their Jurassic ancestry, birds have evolved the past 160 million years. They are winged survivors that tell us how well an ecosystem is doing by how well they can adapt and thrive. It is fascinating to observe the activities of birds and witness the cycles of nesting and migration. Birders learn to visually and musically identity a species by their colorful plumage and rhythmic songs and calls.

Rachel Carson (1907-1964) was an American biologist, ecologist, and author who wrote stories about the science and wonder of wildlife habitat. With her seminal book, *Silent Spring*, she became a legendary catalyst in the global environmental movement. Published in 1962, the popular groundbreaking book alerted to the dangers of uncontrolled use of chemical pesticides and its effects on ecosystems and the food chain. An artist and scientist, she stayed focused on her cause of environmental education and bravely revealed important information and science that changed the status quo. Rachel Carson tapped her intellectual resolve and creative gift for well-informed writing to bring into awareness the need to sustain our natural environment. She fearlessly endeavored to conserve the planet by educating the population. That legacy continues today in the Federal Wildlife Refuges around America that bear her name. Recognizing the therapeutic and restorative qualities of the natural world, she wrote, "There is something infinitely healing in the repeated refrains of nature." A true artist-scientist, Rachel Carson was an environmental pioneer. Today, her legacy continues to inspire a new generation of scientists and concerned citizens working to sustain our planet. The author shared wisdom and a love for nature through education, the art of storytelling, and community activism. Now, more than ever, her words resonate.

Art in nature heals the mind-body-spirit. Creative experience in a natural setting gives us time to reflect and connect to Earth. It opens the senses to new forms of expression. Nature is the model for life and art. Elements of nature inspire the thinker, tinkerer, crafter, writer, and image-maker. Water is a metaphor for expression, the intuitive and intelligent imagination flowing and finding its way to the river of creativity. The substance of water has therapeutic effects, whether submerged in or imagining it, and when we see or listen to it as it flows. The average human body is about 60% water, and the total percentage of water on the planet's surface is about 70%. We are like water. Expressed by philosophers, painters, poets, or musicians, the *moving* flow of water is a universal theme that draws the connection between consciousness and unconsciousness and the deep, pure source from which creativity emerges.

Water is a metaphor for *FLOW*. As an open water swimmer, I love the sensory feel when submerged in a lake or the ocean. It can be warm, fresh, and calm, or cool, salty, and choppy. Swimming in open water is a medium that carries me away, free to float and splash and see things from a different perspective. As a painter, I am inspired by my "swimmer's-eye" view and make watercolors of water and waves in *motion*. My preferred medium of watercolor and using washes lends itself to the wetness and fluidity of this form of expression.

I have witnessed the magic of water, art, and healing as beautifully lived by a breast cancer survivor I met in my expressive arts practice. She collected an origami paper crane at the cancer center every time she had treatment. After gathering a group of the colorful birds, she celebrated the end of her treatment by setting them adrift in the tidal river where they made their way to the ocean, taking flight and the disease with them. During her treatment, the woman had shining optimism about her life and was supported by positive and loving people. The closure of her illness came with the organic ritual of releasing the artful symbols of her healing into the flowing waters, *moving onward and beyond* into a natural environment that she knows and loves. Art + nature + love = healing.

We create environments in natural, social, and cultural habitats, creatively ordering our surroundings for living at home, work, and in the community. The physical place where we are sustained and comfortable is natural habitat. The people and groups we connect with is social habitat. The history and artistic traditions of our local community is cultural habitat. Any habitat can be a creative ecosystem. Home habitat is a personal creative pod and foundation. It's where we experience our most intimate expressions and cultivate a lifestyle. The environments we create and occupy give us grounding and are an important factor in health and well-being. Along with light and color, habitat is impacted by sensory input. The habitat where we create influences how and what we create.

Traveling to a different environment can be a rich source of creative and cultural enrichment. It *moves* energy and expands our world view. Creativity is activated in novel ways when we leave our geographic comfort zone to explore other spaces and places. Going and returning, a journey stimulates the mind-body-spirit. It is a sensory experience, a change in scenery and attitude that gives a different perspective. Traveling by car, boat, plane, train, bike, or foot are roaming modes for creativity in *motion*. Touring or visiting natural places includes boats or campers, or any human-powered method that gets you to that favorite quiet pond or mountain summit. Kayak + SUV + provisions x the great outdoors = ROAD TRIP! Eco-tourism offers opportunities around the globe for visiting exotic natural environments. Travel teaches us about the diverse ecosystems and cultures in a geographic area. The art and architecture of a place are a direct expression of its local resources and natural environment. There is much to see and learn on our planet. The creative journey is just a trip away.

Throughout life, we experience environments and familiar habitats that awaken the senses and inspire wellness. These are the places and everyday environs where we feel a strong resonance and geo-connection. A family home, favorite destination, historic landmark, local community campus, or a vista of nature gives a sense of belonging every time we visit, in the moment or in memory. Where we live and go is our evolving habitat. A creative ecosystem can be a personal oasis, spare room, lively city street, park bench, office cubby, public library, or lakeside camp. An inspiring environment, close to home or beyond the horizon, opens the heart to the wonder and natural beauty of the world.

What is your environment creative wellness?

11: Community Creative Wellness

social sphere, art of relationship, family, partners, pets, friends, neighbors, colleagues, fellowship, groups, organizations, diversity, your tribe, fashion, public venues, social networks, citizen artist, volunteering, activism, community arts, celebration

The community is creative. Our social sphere is a sense of place and connection through belonging to a commonwealth of natural resources, social relationships, and cultural traditions within a population. These are essential to a healthy life and human fulfillment. Community is a beautiful day in the neighborhood, a friendly "hello" that says you're home. Within a local environment, the bonds we share with community make us kin. When we commune we unite, we are alike. I am another you and you are another me.

Factors that create a community are the basic tenets of wellness. This includes respect for diversity, ecological care of natural resources, social and economic justice for all citizens, and living well in a peaceful, nonviolent democracy. These elements of communal living are the social values of Shambhala, a mythical city that Tibetan Buddhists believe is a pure land in the human realm. One cannot actually arrive there, only by karmic affiliation can the city be entered. The enlightened maxim of this great lost society is to live in natural harmony with the qualities of compassion, generosity, mindfulness, and wisdom. The Shambhala model of collective goodwill would work well for any community on the planet.

Cultural diversity enriches the creative ecosystem. Varied backgrounds, beliefs, interests, skills, and points of view foster tolerance and unite people in a beautiful blending of all the ways we are different. Creativity is a unifying act. The arts connect people in a common place and experience. The way we look, dress, act, and celebrate together is how we brand identity within a community. We are citizen artists. Art in a local culture permeates the individual and collective. Natural locations, cultural institutions, public spaces, festivals, fairs, and familiar surroundings are local venues for art-making, art-taking, and art-giving. We make art with the community in classes, workshops, and groups. We take art with the community at events or performances that feature visual art, theatre, music, or narrative. We give art with the community through supporting local arts organizations, joining a collaborative, and volunteering for creative causes to help others. These activities provide entertainment and enrichment. Public art, holiday festivals, group traditions, and educational or historical programs can be peak creative experiences. We are convivial creatures who unite to celebrate our collective creativity. We dance with the flash mob, tailgate grill at the big game, gather for a theatre performance, and volunteer to make the world a better place.

Groups that focus on peer support offer creative fellowship and opportunities for personal growth and connectedness. Along with close relationships and peers, our tribe is a community family where we can be ourselves and share like-minded values and cultural traditions. The earliest humans survived within a social clan. We evolved because we felt empathy toward others and the need to better our mutual existence. Studies show that having social connection is a major factor in our ability to recover from illness and trauma, and it is an important indicator of longevity and happiness. The interpersonal input and output in a group is a catalyst for creativity. The interactive and participatory dynamics of listening, looking, learning, and improvising with people expands personal and communal perspectives. It is the joy of *moving* from Me to We.

In the safety of a group, emotions and fears can be released by expressing what is personally difficult through a common process. Clinical support groups use creative therapies to teach skills for managing stress and physical symptoms by engaging in experiential activities. Participants expect interaction with peers, but what happens during the process is spontaneous. The goal is to offer therapy tools for personal growth that nurture creativity. In my expressive arts practice, I facilitate creativity workshops in both clinical and non-clinical settings. Visual arts and writing with a group are excellent ways to increase confidence and learn skills that can be enjoyed ongoing. These programs are locally based and provide consistent support to participants. I've witnessed transformative experiences as people find and express their creative true voice. This form of interactive participation is affirming and empowering for the individual and the group.

Our social sphere is an intimate network of relations and relationships. It includes family, partners, friends, pets, colleagues, and neighbors. We are social animals. A social sphere can have little universes of like-minded fans and followers with layers of connectivity. This is the community mosaic where the art of relationship is expressed. Social networking is a way we connect with people online. Technology has dramatically increased the ability to be in touch without physical touch. Pictures and messages posted by family and friends from afar on social media sites show babies grown, food eaten, and vacations taken. We can see it all in real-time with a video device. It virtually expands sociability. We glimpse the daily creative musings of a social ecosystem in our personal newsfeed. With just one click, we share with a crowd and connect to a broader community conversation.

The twentieth century American pop artist Andy Warhol (1928-1987) was an oracle when he said in the 1970s, "Everyone will have 15 minutes of fame." With his genius for expressing the popular culture, Andy would absolutely be a creative influencer in social media today with his trend-setting pop images, weirdly wonderful wit, and that wild white hair. Fame is a community concept that can be driven by creativity, and more importantly, originality. The internet gives everyone an editorial voice. Sometimes it can drive people to chase notice, for better or worse. Mostly, it is an important platform for the aspiring visual artist, performer, photographer, writer, activist, or intellectual who posts original ideas and creative works.

For as much as we communicate in the digital ether, there is still nothing that opens the senses and touches the heart like a friendly voice on the phone, or better, visiting a friend and seeing their smile. Communicating with all the senses is how social relationships reach their fullest creative potential. Friends are a gift of community. Kindred in spirit, they are special people who expand our creativity and circle of love. Friends are an abundant source of play and appreciate our quirky, wonderful ways. They give hugs of advice and a sounding board for our deep thoughts, abstract ideas, and tender emotions. Time shared with friends grounds us in the feeling of belonging to an extended social clan. They are a community family. Friendship is a peak creative experience. Friends form and inform our timeline, wherever that special person is on the planet. Life is enriched with the confidence of fellowship. Your BFF, best friend forever, is always there. A longtime friend shares the artifacts of a relationship and sameness of spirit that bonds and gives comfort. As we age, we don't easily make new old friends and spend more time cherishing the memories of those who have passed on from our lives. Friends are our most creative social resource. Through good times and bad, when in need, a friend is a friend, indeed.

Being a citizen artist in your tribe is a way to be original while being part of a peer group. Differentness is okay. Your tribe is a modern family that shares like-minded values and accepts you unconditionally. The way we dress reflects how we self-identify in our community. Fashion, for a stylish example, is both a personal and shared form of expression. Our mode can be a uniform or anti-uniform, whatever works and defines character and style. The global fashion culture is a collective unconscious of what's in vogue at the moment. From the street to the runway to the street again, the cycles of fashion follow the perfect little black dress or up-to-date power suit. A great thing about fashion is that a power suit can be one-piece, two-piece, three-piece, dressy, casual, jump, bathing, or birthday. If it suits you, it's a power suit. Clothing is a medium for freedom of speech and creative pride in our appearance. What we wear and how we wear it is a primal source of visual expression. The body is a blank canvas for artisan apparel, jewelry, and accessories. The art of tattoo and make-up decorates the body in the spirit of the tribe. Hairdos and hemlines, footwear and sportswear, fashion is how we present ourselves in a particular social sphere. It sets the creative style for how we communicate and associate.

Personal style follows or sets the trends and is a fashion-forward medium for self-expression that changes with the seasons. The legendary New York Times fashion photographer Bill Cunningham (1929-2016) was known for his animated pictures of people wearing high fashion on the street and celebrities and socialites at stylish events. He documented the fashion industry for over six decades and observed the cycles of style being invented and reinvented more than a few times. His photographs brilliantly captured well-dressed people in their cultural habitat. The fashion tribe looking good in the latest looks. With his upbeat perspective, Bill mused, "That's what fashion is all about! Hope of something new." Hope springs eternal, time to buy new shoes!

Creative citizenry taps people-powered collaboration for the good of all. Team creativity. Locally, the region where we live is a rich source of economic innovation and inspiration. Businesses and occupations are creative relative to the local population and resources. In a community work environment, we collaborate and endeavor towards a mutual goal that sustains the group. People being productive with pride and purpose builds social capital. Labor is not always loved, however, it is enjoyed when supported by workmates who know how to solve problems, laugh at jokes, and get the job done with integrity and friendship. It is the responsibility of companies to promote a healthy culture in the workplace. This common sense practice results in a productive workforce and profitable company. A work environment without wellness is toxic and affects the entire socio-economic spectrum, from the laborer to the CEO. A creative company values the health and well-being of the employees and their families, promotes diversity, and supports every worker's needs while producing revenues.

People working and growing together is the common goal of a community garden. Local lands in urban, suburban, or rural areas are organized and cultivated cooperatively. Individuals or groups maintain plots for growing food and flowers for families or community members, as well as for the pleasure of digging and weeding. Gardeners plant and labor collaboratively to nurture optimal growing conditions for the group. Every participant is responsible for keeping their plot and using the best practices. In my local community garden and most places in Maine, organic gardening practices are generally used. As a community of gardeners, we help each other learn cultivation techniques, offer remedies for pests, and cheer the season of abundance. Shared social and environmental values are the foundation of public gardens and community-supported agriculture. The process builds citizenry with opportunities for schools, farmers markets, and agricultural groups that involve peer goals and education.

Social entrepreneurs use innovative strategies for solving community-based problems and supporting economic development by investing in local resources and people. Locally and globally, humanitarian and nonprofit organizations work towards their missions to improve communities and serve the needs of a population at a grassroots level. This cultivates common ground for the common good.

The health, social, and cultural needs of a community, and working to serve those populations, drives the missions of nonprofit organizations. Creative experience is inspired by what we value and passionately care about. Volunteering to be part of something we believe in and rolling up our sleeves to help is a wonderful way to find ourselves by losing ourselves in service to others. Becoming an active volunteer with like-minded people working for a good cause teaches new skills and expands our social sphere. It feels good because volunteering empowers purpose, boosts self-esteem, increases energy, utilizes talents, and activates feelings of compassion and altruism. There is a euphoric vitality that comes with the "helper's high" as endorphins are stimulated and released by the reward of work well done. Volunteering is a way to be an upstander versus a bystander. This means making a stand and showing up to take action towards positive change.

Involvement allows us to lean into our cause. Activism is creative. It's an opportunity and privilege to serve. Activism for the greater good takes just one person working to make a difference. The creative activist is a voice of truth that advocates new awareness and action through grassroots, volunteer-supported initiatives. Activists act in response to social, political, cultural, or ecological issues. Throughout history, the world would never have changed for the better without a little acting up. Criticize by creating. This is often the way of the artists, scientists, teachers, thinkers, doers, lovers, parents, warriors, and wise people who are the knowers and keepers of our best qualities. They are the heroes who create and sustain community well-being for the good of all citizens and the planet. In its highest form, community activism is a nonviolent initiative that informs and improves the human condition.

Group music-making and performative arts build social connections and raise empathy through the lens of creativity. The sopranos, altos, tenors, and basses are all in harmony with each other, who are in sync with the choral director and musical score. In concert, we honor the people we love, practice faith, share ideas, and celebrate gifts of the spirit. Music is powerful when our voices are singing together. The wellness benefits associated with singing in a group come from the collective vibrational experience and how we listen and respond to others. Singing anthems in a community unites the singers and listeners through music that is meaningful and symbolic. Community anthems that inspire hope are a shared peak creative experience.

Art for social change, community activism, and the desire to improve life for the greater good can inform a life's work. The late, great Pete Seeger (1919-2014) was an American singer and song writer. An authentic citizen artist and activist, he believed in the power of expressing creative true voice and people singing together. With a banjo, guitar, and collection of treasured folksongs, he raised community consciousness through music and taught us that we all have a voice and it is valued. The musician believed in the unifying power of music and was a master of facilitating the individual's creative voice in harmony with the collective. Now iconic in the American soundscape, his much-loved music is often a simple story that shows a better way. He created community through shared music and activated like-minded and different-minded people to join in the chorus and be part of something bigger than the individual. Pete empowered people through the power of art and sang with creative true voice for social and environmental justice. He celebrated freedom of the individual for the greater good and inspired music lovers and change-makers. One artist's voice, rising up, can create positive change. Sing for change, all over this land!

A wise African proverb says, "It takes a village to raise a child." A life-sustaining society that is good for the individual is good for the population. Sustainability is creative. It's a generative and regenerative mode of productive living that values the individual and group with respect for the Earth's resources. It is how the tribe survives and thrives. We must co-create and grow together to sustain a good life for ourselves and the collective.

Like a village raising a child together, mentors are fundamental to teaching, learning, and growing in every community. These are people who share skills and knowledge to uplift others. Mentors are the teachers, coaches, friends, relatives, and nurturing relationships that help us achieve our highest potential. They believe in our talents, brilliant ideas, and dreams.

Mentors guide us in an area of interest that needs development such as the arts, education, health, athletics, domesticity, parenting, community leadership, or spirituality. They support personal growth and success at any stage and in all aspects of life. When the student is ready, the mentor appears. It's important to recognize the enrichment value of mentors, those strong individuals who help us become our best selves by affirming and *motivating* creativity.

A creative community builds immunity, because what's healthy for an individual is good for the population. Community art connects people. Public art introduces new ideas, highlights conflicts, and helps us learn, communicate, and heal together. Wellness happens when we become part of the group consciousness, the individual merging with the collective, Me to We. A caring community is good medicine. In my local nonprofit work, I've collaborated with young volunteer artists from local schools to make art cards and origami cranes for local cancer patients and health groups. The small artistic offering says to the person receiving it that the community cares and is thinking about you. Art-making, art-taking, and art-giving are powerful remedies that nurture wellness and loving kindness.

Throughout history, during times of social revolution and tragedy, citizen artists have *moved* their voices to sing anthems, pens to write the truth, cameras to record the moment, paintbrushes to express beauty and hope, and bodies to dance with the rhythms of life. Creativity helps people in times of uncertainty and sorrow. Terrorist acts, mass shootings, environmental disasters, war crimes, social injustice, or a global pandemic. World events *motivate* us to unite in collective compassion and grief by sharing stories and expressing the inexpressible in a common language. In recent decades, the arts provided ways to respond to traumatic and unprecedented historic events. These are community arts and healing initiatives that inspired me on my journey to write this book: *Names Project AIDS Memorial Quilt; Vietnam Veterans Memorial Wall; 911 Tribute In Light at the World Trade Center;* and *12-12-12 Concert for Hurricane Sandy Relief.*

As I write these words, there is a public health crisis affecting the entire global population. The COVID virus has caused significant social and emotional changes for everyone. We need to adapt to a new normal to mitigate the spread of the virus. Distancing and not seeing facial expressions because of masks is contrary to our social nature. We are convivial creatures. We like to kiss, hug, talk, and be close without restrictions. The viral pandemic has exacerbated an existing mental health epidemic. We've experienced unprecedented emotional stress and anxiety because of loss of life, lack of income and supplies, isolation and shifts in social freedom, and the confusion and uncertainty of the times. Now is the time to compassionately *move* forward, from Me to We. Let's take care of ourselves and each other. The global community must unite and utilize all our resources and goodwill with social justice and fairness for all. We are getting better together.

As the pandemic ramped up in early 2020, our creative resilience shined a light on our humanity during some of the darkest moments. In neighborhoods and digital networks, we invented novel ways to connect with loved ones and the community while being apart. With love, compassion, and creativity, we fought an unseen and unknown enemy that united our healing intentions. All over the world, people *moved* to create music, images, and words that reflect our humanity and shared empathy. We rise as citizens artists. We perform music to comfort and anthems of hope from balconies, desktops, and couches at home. Dancers keep *moving*, and yoga instructors provide do-it-yourself videos to show us how to stay active. Visual artists capture the moment with inspiring pictures and healing symbols. Writers go deep to craft language for the new paradigm. We are innovating business and social interactions that will forever change how we work, learn, and live communally. Our everyday creativity is how we originate and communicate during challenging times. Art is a response we can all do to improve ourselves and the world. Human creativity is a ready remedy. When we *move* as a community toward a positive resolution, it is like a wave that flows and energizes in a deluge that washes away the woe. These years will mark our collective timeline as the moment when the global community came together for the common good. It takes a village to heal the world, indeed.

Consider the friends, artists, teachers, mentors, heroes, and change-makers who have impacted your community life. What values and ideals do you share? Tap those creative influences to create a change in your community. Work for a cause and share your special talents and skills, locally or globally. Your creative true voice is needed to make a positive difference in the world.

What is your community creative wellness?

12: Home Creative Wellness

artist-in-residence, living space, sense of place, native habitat, homesteading, homemaking, domestic arts, shelter in place, organizing, interior design, home improvement, home office, hobbies, handicrafts, gardening, cooking, creative refuge

The home is creative. Wherever we physically live, home is a sense of place and belonging. It is where we dwell well, and can be couched in creature comforts, relaxed with our feet up. The artist-in-residence likes to be in their native habitat. Beginning with the structural design and arrangement of living space, the art of domesticity is expressed with ambient lighting, colors and textures, cozy areas, functional rooms, and elements of nature. It is the creative ecosystem where we sleep, store possessions, cook food, wash clothes, work on hobbies, and spend intimate time alone and with others. It's where our stuff is and happens, a creative refuge for taking shelter and self-care.

Working in the right livelihood, we make home a nurturing and sustaining environment that reflects our interests and basic needs. It is a primary comfort zone that blends social and ecological spheres informed by life experience and geographic location. We have an instinctive need to inhabit a space and feel safe in a familiar habitat. Whether residing alone or with others, we need somewhere to be ourselves, a personal container that gives an order to the chaos of living. Home is where we shelter in place with all that is needed to survive and thrive. The concept of sheltering in place gives a new awareness of what it takes to sustain basic needs and what we value most. Sheltering well requires common sense and good planning. As people learn what it takes to hunker down, they find creative ways to manage resources and have enough on hand in the pantry to get by. Being content and self-contained in a place allows for taking stock and understanding what maintains health and feeds the soul. It is a way to get creative about basic living. Sustainability starts at home, where we recycle, reinvent, and refresh our lives.

There are different homes where we reside. Fundamentally, we are fortunate to have an adequate shelter that is affordable and supports basic survival. We all need a home base to be grounded and nurtured. This varies depending on our timeline. Living in the right environment supports wellness and increases lifespan. We live our years in a childhood home, college dorm, that first great apartment, an adult abode, or nursing home. Some people have large palatial homes while others have none. It is important that having a home and sense of place is not taken for granted. A homeless individual or family does not have a place to dwell and feel comfort. Homelessness is a negative health factor and social stigma that can be a hard cycle to break with the barriers of mental illness and poverty. However, it can be a personal transition to a new home life. In the modern world no one should go without shelter. Collectively, our creative ingenuity and empathy can ameliorate this social problem.

There is a new trend to build micro houses, tiny efficiencies for one or two occupants that are on wheels or in a stationary location. This kind of housing is helping homeless people. In urban areas, tiny house sanctuaries are being set up on community land with agencies that provide social service support. Tiny houses are a social and architectural concept that requires people to pare down to the basics. It advocates for sustainable and simple living. This mode of abode appeals to a broad spectrum of homesteaders, from the back-to-the-earth folks to urban renegades. Tiny houses are incredibly cute and cleverly designed to provide all that is needed at a minimum. Imagine your entire home in less than 500 cubic feet. It is a concept that requires abundant imagination and innovation, which is why the trend is so popular with free spirits who want to downsize.

People often live with roommates in a shared home. Many people are housed with intergenerational family members, especially as the baby boomers are aging. Modern living requires creatively adapting to the extended responsibilities and needs related to caring for others. Housing and living costs are expensive which determines the way we share our home resources or live independently. Many young adults are staying close to the nest with parents because they can't afford to be on their own. They are often paying off college debt or looking for work, and it's still comfy to be at home. It is common for modern families to live with aging relatives and extended family members for economic and social support. Whether living solo or with a clan, it is important to have a personal creative refuge within a home environment.

Humans evolved because we are successful homesteaders able to make the most of our resources to facilitate health and comfort. It hasn't always been easy for humans living in communal conditions. Our collective creative will is key to survival. Prehistoric cave dwellers and civilizations had to work and share together. They utilized their ingenuity and problem-solving skills to create the fundamental elements necessary for living. No television or wifi in the cave in those days, early humans were creatively occupied with day to day survival. The home was a community-supported experience or the tribe didn't survive. Its success depended on the creative ideas and innovations of every clan member. The remaining artifacts remind us that home is a universal center for cultural tradition. Pottery, fabric, art, tools, furniture, jewelry, and ornamental objects have enriched communal living since the beginning of human companionship.

Communal homesteading, past and present, involves common values and collaboration to create abundance in the home and garden. Homesteaders sustain and share resources by working together to make a good life for the group. It takes a village. Today a new generation of homesteaders are making homes on land, where they grow food and work to sustain their environment. They are young farmers, artisans, naturalists, environmentalists, survivalists, families, or groups of like-minded people who cultivate land and community. These homesteaders live cooperatively by sharing land, housing, or a neighborhood. The values of resourcefulness, simplicity, independence, respect for nature, and healthy living are why homesteading is a way to wellness.

Native habitat is a personal ecosystem that stimulates the senses and nurtures homeostasis. A vista of nature, wind chimes that catch the breeze, smells of supper cooking, a cozy chair that beckons, the deluxe home entertainment system. These are creature comforts that make home the place to be. We upscale and downscale a home environment to reflect our work in progress lives. How and where we work often reflects how and where we domicile. "Home sweet office" is more common as we redesign our modern lifestyles to be more home-based and balanced. This is an important trend because time is the key to wellness. A home workspace can be liberating and reflect personal creative interests. It is a familiar environment that makes work feel more like a day off. Working at home cuts down on the time and stress of commuting. This is how companies can support the wellness of their employees. Even a few days a week, working from home reduces stress, increases productivity, and minimizes the monotony of rush hour commuting that steals time and creative energy. More time = more creativity = more productivity.

The domestic arts help manage home and hearth with utility and craftsmanship. Homemaking is a perfect metaphor for everyday creativity. Methods for ordering, cleaning, and caring for the home are challenges that inspire homemakers to think, make, and innovate. Homemaking happens because need is the mother of invention. We creatively craft solutions for performing daily tasks, organizing space, and grooming a habitat. We like things to function, look nice, and feel comfortable so we *move* and rearrange our stuff. Having a tidy and organized space makes extra room for a creative activity. Feng shui is a philosophical practice that helps orient a work or home area in the most auspicious energetic manner. This organic order considers how a physical space and the things within it are oriented to the natural environment in balance with personal energy and the Universe. It is a beautiful, practical way to clean up and minimize clutter.

Resourceful homemakers craft artisan products for getting chores done. Herbal soaps to calm and clean, old-fashioned and new-fashioned brooms, decorative baskets and pottery, and aromatic candles are handcrafted classics. Our artistic passion for homemaking has produced kitchen cookware, gadgets, home accessories, and appliances that work like a charm. Our creative approach to domesticity can be extreme with all the fixings, bells, and whistles, or simply styled, understated, and utilitarian. Making and enjoying a cozy lifestyle with all the little homey touches and good food and infusions in season is a peak creative experience. A bowl of apples, a bouquet of flowers, fresh-baked bread, homemade fish chowder, and a table set for a feast. The art of enjoying abundance, let's eat!

Domesticity inspires making things by hand that are beautiful and practical. Spinning, weaving, knitting, hooking, stitching, and sewing are traditional fiber arts that produce functional and fanciful items. Often, skills are passed from a parent or mentor to the next generation of crafters. Our most personal stories are told by the threads that connect us. We cherish the quilts, baby bonnets, tapestries, and embroidered tablecloths lovingly crafted by the homemaker's hand. Designed for utility and decor, handmade baskets and pottery represent the most practical and beautiful art traditions of domestic living. The finest pieces of folk art were touched by the hands of an artist-crafter. The carpenter crafts furniture and restores useful items for household needs. Home welcomes the one-of-a-kind. Handicraft engages the brain-eyes-hands function in a productive activity. The art of crafting is a mindful process. Being self-aware and self-expressive builds maker-confidence. This artistry feels like a happy hobby, because the practice of mindfulness reduces stress. Handicraft is handy and healthy in the home, and enjoyed by the maker and user.

The creative collector considers home when gathering treasures that reflect a personal aesthetic or interest. Anything can be collected, from cameras to fossils, and displayed within the home environs. We are hobbyists who love antiques, cars, toys, books, ceramics, clothing, fine art, and eccentric and eclectic things. Our home collections reflect our creative individualism. We collect memories by handcrafting scrapbooks and photo albums into works of art that illustrate the stories of our lives. Personal items and objects articulate who we are and what we love. In the home, a collector shares space with the objects collected. A prized collection can be a visual focal point in the design of a room. Some of the most well-designed home spaces are the shelves, closets, and cabinets that hold our collections and stuff in an organized scheme, or not. Home indulges the human habit to make order from chaos, or not.

Home is where we nurture and grow. Indoor or outdoor gardening brings greenery to living. We cultivate plants and trees for food and beauty. Horticulture is a home-based way to practice mindfulness and reduce stress. Simple indoor gardening enriches and adds color to an interior environment. There is satisfaction in wintering geraniums inside, pruning and directing them toward the light, or starting a tomato seed on a kitchen window sill in the spring and planting it in the vegetable garden when the ground warms. Home gardening fosters an awareness of the natural environment and familiarity with the blooming cycles of each potted house plant and perennial in the garden. For creative cultivators, it gives a sense of place and purpose and can be a place to retreat with landscaped areas and meditation space or a grassy spot that invites sitting and simply being. Flowers, vegetables, and fruit trees enhance environs and offer colorful possibilities for making fresh floral bouquets and seasonal fare.

A dedicated home gardener plans growing space and planting times. The process of gardening with hands and knees in the dirt, nurturing and cultivating, seeing things flourish and die in natural cycles is a peak creative experience. Cold zone perennial gardeners know this miraculous cycle of growth. We see hardy plants find warmth in spring, thrive, bloom, and then rest dormant in winter, sometimes under feet of snow. A perennial garden in mid-winter versus high growing season makes a home gardener passionate about cultivation. Warm zone gardeners have other challenges and can grow and harvest throughout the year. We are fortunate when skilled and devoted horticulturalists open their cultivated environments to visitors for seasonal garden tours. The property where a master gardener has developed the landscape, sometimes over many decades, is amazing to experience in full flower and through all seasons of the year.

From garden to kitchen, domestic arts in the home touch the senses in ways that speak to our heritage and love of making things from scratch. Wildcrafted herbs infuse teas and soups. Garden fruits become handcrafted jellies, pickles, and sauces for the pantry. In many American rural communities, local agricultural fairs feature what can be considered the Olympics of homemade products crafted from locally grown produce in season. Traditional fairs have contests with wonderful displays of culinary artistry that include categories for pies, bread, preserved foods, vinegar, and wines. The pavilions housing these events at big fairs are alive with the colors and textures of homegrown fruits and vegetables and homemade delights. The conversations of proud growers and makers enliven the exhibition hall, though likely no prize-winning recipes are shared. Generally, if you are at an event and there is a pie contest volunteer to judge. Someone needs to taste-test to determine who wins the blue ribbon.

A kitchen is the heart of every creative home. It is a thoroughfare of activity and shared experiences. Here is where the domestic arts find their stage. A typical kitchen is the center of home life, whether in a small urban condo or a large country farm house. For the happy homemaker, the kitchen is general headquarters. Kitchen tables are the all-purpose home surface for school work, the sewing machine, playing cards, and any project or activity that needs a spot. Home kitchens facilitate our ability to provide food. It's the place where we make and break bread. Cooking is love made visible. The activities and aromas of a cook in the kitchen give a warm feeling to home that awakens the senses with anticipation of a tasty meal. To cook and be

cooked for, both are peak creative experiences that tickle the taste buds. Food in the home, slow or fast, on any weeknight or feasting holiday, is the comfort of the familiar. The culinary alchemy of a homemade catch-all soup or salad, spiced just right, is what creativity tastes like. The harmonious home is delicious. Let me share my *Recipe for Creative Wellness*:
- *one part inspiration*
- *one part motivation*
- *one part creation*
- *one part magic*
- *mix well and sprinkle with love*

Castle or cottage, apartment or condo, den or nest - home where we survive and thrive, a place like no other to rest and recreate, celebrate and create. Creativity is how we make it a home sweet home, every day.

What is your home creative wellness?

13: Language Creative Wellness

internal or external language, verbal or written communication, sensory mediums, speaking, listening, gesturing, vernacular, media, narrative, storytelling, words, reading, writing, imagery, symbols, emoticons, humor, dreams, creative affirmations

Language is creative. It's a basic impulse to self-express, communicate, and relate. We systematically organize thoughts and feelings into language using all the senses. Language functions as a delivery system for all forms of expression. Words, images, symbols, sounds, and signs are primary methods of communicating. There are many forms of language that inform and interpret life. Creativity is an experiential language that fuses communication skills with our thoughts, emotions, and experiences. All language is expression in *motion,* externally with other people and internally with ourselves.

External language is how we talk with each other. It reflects the diversity and expansiveness of the world, and is informed by the vast information resources available globally in historic annuals, books, periodicals, blogs, journals, and visual media. The etymology of words is evolving right before our twenty-first-century eyes and ears as we learn to communicate in a new global society. Education uses multimedia audio and visual technologies to implement learning and language. Newspapers, magazines, and print and digital media saturate and influence our daily sensory experience. Televisions, radios, computers, tablets, and phones are tools that facilitate 24/7 language creative wellness. Social media is a common platform for modern communication that gives a creative voice to anyone who posts, shares, comments, or reacts. The media of external language includes visual arts, graphics, photography, sound-tracks, videos, memes, and narratives.

Internal language is how we talk with self. This is the creative true voice telling its story. It is an intuitive way to understand and express thoughts and feelings that is subjective. Listen, it is the mind-body-spirit talking, the call that says, "I am creative". This is the realm of the psyche, intuition, and dreams. Our inner dialogue speaks in words, images, and sensory responses. It is the things we tell ourselves and what we perceive with the mind's eye. Internal language expresses what we know and believe. It informs external communications and actions. It is the wellspring of imagination, mindfulness, and creative flow. Having a healthy inner dialogue is essential to self-awareness and self-healing.

The way we express language, the things we think and feel internally, that we want to say externally, can be prompted by an experiential creative process. Like using our hands to hold a printed book and tactically embracing it with discovery; or handwriting a poem passionately with a pen to paper. The eyes and hands kinetically engage the brain. The brain-eyes-hands function is key to learning and communicating. Humans like to *move* their energy and make their mark or match. Writing by hand enlivens the brain to record language in a visual form. It is a complex task that stimulates the brain to coordinate cognitive, motor, and neuromuscular processes. We tend to remember things when handwritten, and it helps us learn. Printing and writing by hand at an early age are important to understanding the structure of language. It primes young students to be better at two-handed typing on a computer keyboard. Just a thought for computer-only writers; pen to paper is an exhilarating, organic process for creating language.

In part, this book was crafted from the over 4000 hand-written and drawn 4 x 6-inch index cards I made to collect my ideas and research for writing the narrative. Going through the chaos of the cards and putting them in order was like a big puzzle. With thousands of hours of persistent work and word-crafting, those notes grew into the language on these pages. After a decade of writing and rewriting, it is interesting to look back at the thought-charged cards. They are a plethora of passionately scribed ideas, research notes, evolving concepts, questions, reminders, and pictographs. Some of the cards are written in such an energetic script that, as I recorded them, it was like chasing the idea with my mind's hand. I couldn't relate the same energetic process with a computer. Writing and drawing by hand keep us in touch with our native creativity and the fertile flow that *motivates* the expression of language.

Oral and written stories are intrinsic to communication and the common ways we relate. Language skills and oral storytelling evolved simultaneously as prehistoric humans developed tools and culture. We learn to tell stories instinctually and through the language arts, those most-loved school subjects of reading, spelling, literature, and composition. As storytellers, we find our creative true voice with a style and point-of-view that is personal and collective. Stories are how we learn, share memories, recount histories, and foster relatedness. They help us understand abstract concepts and the realities of life through narratives woven by the teller, word by word. Modern community storytelling circles range from an intimate fireside chat to social networking with multitudes. We can be active listeners in diverse genres. Stories teach universal truths, literally and metaphorically. They give a perspective of the human experience that informs and inspires, enlightens and expands, breaks silence and gives voice to ideas. Stories are observations of life in any language medium that tell what we think, feel, and imagine. Artistically and culturally, they relate what is relatable.

We all have stories to tell. Free verse is our free will. Poets know this. They know how to meditate on words and rhythms and mind-craft their expression with cadence and emotion. Any junkyard poet will tell you of the pain and pleasure released through the metaphorical play of word and phrase. Poetry is a type of response art, a narrative interpretation of our thoughts and feelings. Written or read, it often says the unsayable. Poetry is a primal impulse to announce, share, and express. It is the verse of love and war, beauty and despair. To write a little and say a lot is the way of the poet. This requires contemplation, verbal skill, and a strong feeling heart. A song or ballad is sung poetry. A poem set to music is a powerful medium for storytelling. Broadway, pop, folk, rock, and rap give us the musical poems we often repeat and playback in our lyric memory. Poetry is the power of words that resonate with universal rhythm.

Writing is therapeutic and often used in expressive arts to support mental health and long-term illness. Writing for wellness engenders a cathartic experience that opens creative flow and self-awareness. This promotes deep self-care. Free writing is a method to clear the mind and speak with creative true voice. It doesn't require any formal grammar or structure, just a language response in your own style. Speaking about what speaks to you. It is a way to write about thoughts and feelings without any self-judgment or criticism. To write your right.

A journal or diary is a good way to explore the flow of free writing. It is a personal space to express thoughts and feelings, tell stories, make lists, sketch, and meditate. A journal is an excellent resource for life review, recording memories, and reading about your resilience. Oh, the wondrous possibilities of a blank page! Journal writing prompts the why, what, when, and where of the day and a lifetime. Write about everything and nothing. Just *move* your pencil on the paper and don't stop writing. Trust the flow. Fifteen minutes of writing a day exercises cognitive function, reduces stress, and promotes self-expression in a practice that can be deeply meditative and emotionally balancing. Personal narrative is an ongoing creative practice and a work in progress. There is always something to write about. Whatever the writing style or process, aspiring writers know that good writing happens when ideas are well-organized and presented in words that are enjoyable to read. It takes a great deal of writing to be a good writer.

Recording your dreams is an interesting process for journaling. It's a first thing in the morning writing gig when the motifs and metaphors are captured while still in memory. As crazy as they can sometimes be, dreams help us better understand our psyche and signal what is necessary for conscious change. Dreams are a metaphoric language and a continuation of consciousness. The mind is always awake. We spend an average of two hours dreaming each night. Thoughts suppressed during waking appear as symbols and scenarios that can bring insight and fright. REM is the *rapid eye movement* that occurs when the eyes are closed during deep sleep. It is when most dreaming happens. In theory, this form of sleep is a way that we psychologically heal and consolidate information, past and present, and for some, the future. REM sleep helps build neural connections, particularly in visual areas, and is known to boost creativity. Dreaming helps us solve problems, understand emotional needs, and visualize desires. When recording a dream, the interpretation is less important unless you know the meaning. Just be fluid and write about it or make a sketch. Over time, dream journal entries may provide patterns of behavioral awareness that shine a light on the psychological dynamics and aspects of our lives that require attention.

Through the language of sleep, a dream-worker creatively sets the stage for the emergence of ideas and insights. Dreams communicate psychic information. You never know what the language of dreams may reveal, even though the metaphors can be mind-meltingly weird. People at the end-of-life often experience extraordinary pre-death dreams that help them put their lives into perspective, heal relationships, and affirm a higher power. A lucid dreamer, Albert Einstein mused about a dream that helped him conceive his general theory of relativity. He described it, "Like a giant die making an indelible impress, a huge map of the Universe outlined itself in one clear vision." Write or sketch your night dreams and daydreams, and let the rich internal language of the creative unconscious open a pathway to conscious living.

Reading is a fundamental and fun way to experience language. A book is language's best friend. Lovers of language read and write books. Volumes of stories and histories, fiction and nonfiction, books are a repository of the human story. Books are words made into an experience. Reading a book engages the imagination as words form pictures in our mind and we interpret details of the ideas or themes presented. Like a pebble that transforms the still water, a good book excites new ways of thinking, doing, and being. The creative mind physically enters a book where it goes places and meets new people, learns fresh insights, and imagines in the realm of fantasy. Reading can be an individual or group experience. Book clubs and reading groups connect like-minded readers in a social exchange of ideas and conversations about topics of shared interest. Reading is a wonderful example of art-taking because a reader experiences the author's words through their own creative lens. The imagination makes reading very visual. It's a cultural treasure that allows us to go deeply into a subject and expand knowledge and experience. Deep reading, without hyperlinks or distractions, is a way to read for pleasure rather than for information or in a social manner. The immersion of deep reading allows the brain to focus on the nuances of language and visual metaphors. A good read is a medium for deep flow, a peak creative experience that draws us in and keeps us *moving* across the pages.

Societally, if we are to keep true to our collective true voice, we need to ensure the future of writing and reading books in all their physical and electronic forms. Books are humanity's common record. It is important to support local booksellers and libraries. The hub of language culture in any community, these are places where creative minds can physically explore books and information. The reader-book relationship is personal. As reader-seekers know, there is something thrilling about looking around your favorite book venue for an interesting read. A thrift sale, the town library, and the bookstores you meet in life - we find books and books find us, often when we need them to transform our intellectual and emotional perspectives.

Physical language gets us *moving* and connecting with others. Drama and improvisation are traditional group storytelling methods that engage acting and gesture. Performance brings an audience together in a shared experience through an animated exchange of language. Gesture is a physical language with its own parts of speech that signals what we are thinking and feeling. Body language can be very visual and expressive. Gesture is a primal form of symbolic communication between species, our creature language. Behavior is communication. Somewhere in the evolution of time, a smiling face and wave of the hand became a friendly hello, and an enraged brow and clenched fist broadcast a hostile attitude. Sign language is a very rich form of communication used instead of acoustically spoken language that involves layers of meaning. Tactile and visual signing methods help a mute or deaf person to communicate language. A signer makes gestures using their hands, arms, and body movements in sync with facial expressions to speak with a full voice. The human body can brilliantly express language using touch and physical symbols. Again, the hands and eyes stimulate elements of expression.

We speak using common words with different linguistic styles. Our phraseology, how we organize and choose words, is as unique as we are. It makes conversation a verbal intercourse or discourse. Oral, written, or signed, communication requires understanding the intrinsic structure of a language in various forms. Language is a learning medium, and knowing a second language helps us better understand other cultures. Accents and patterns of vocabulary evolve through local vernacular and colloquialisms with distinctive native genres. "Ayuh, people from away think Mainers talk wicked funny." In perfect slang or syntax, there is beauty and humor in dialect.

Humor helps us be better humans. The language of humor inspires laughter, smiles, giggles, guffaws, hearty roars, and sometimes tears. Humor is a peak creative experience because it feels good to laugh and let go of inhibitions with comic relief. Sometimes a deep uplifting belly laugh can release a little pee or fart. Laughing requires us to be present in the moment. It is a physical language in response to the pleasure of cerebral humor. The funny bone tickled. A healthy laugh can relieve stress, aid digestion, support respiratory function, lower blood pressure, boost the immune system, and improve mood. Smiling is a symptom of wellness. Humor is a happy stimulus. Laughter is the positive physiological and psychological response. It feels good because it activates dopamine in the brain which triggers a release of the body's feel-good endorphins. Humor lowers levels of cortisol, the stress hormone. Ask a happy old-timer and they'll say that having a sense of humor makes longevity all the more fun. There is powerful medicine in mirth, even though laughter can be contagious. A little snicker or satirical wit can accomplish the placebo effect of improved physical health and well-being. We chuckle alone or howl with others. Laughter yoga is a way to group laugh. Funny physical creative wellness, it makes me laugh just imagining the process. Goofball ideas or strange irony, humor is a primal human expression, a universal language that communicates our silly side. Humor dispels grumpy moods and makes us vulnerable to surprise, improvisation, and enjoyment. Whatever the ailment, a little humor can lift spirits, even when it's no laughing matter. Life has its ups and downs, sadness and euphoria. We live through the best and worst times and wit makes everything lighter. Like a vacuum cleaner, humor is one of the few things that is better when it sucks. Having a good sense of humor can be a happy and very funny way to wellness.

Letters, numbers, lines, colors, graphics, pictorial representations, and gestures are visual forms of language. We have an innate ability to recognize and interpret common symbols, motifs, and icons. We see and communicate visually, whether it's an image or facial expression in the flesh. Visual elements of language are some of the most recognized imagery in our consciousness and unconsciousness. The visual language we create with our bodies facilitates individual expression and tells a lot about us. We use illustrated interpretations of written language to communicate every day. For millennia, alphabets and hieroglyphics have depicted a collective visual method for communicating in a common language. From a Mayan glyph to a Helvetica font, visual representations of language evolved to communicate words and ideas, and function as the practical parts that form information.

Symbols and pictograms are a psychological language with the capacity to communicate efficiently and immediately. They are part of a universal illustrated lexicon that transcends text and speaks to a unified culture. Emojis are a modern visual language that expresses what we think and do, and most importantly, how we feel. Happy faces, big hearts, a full wine glass, or hands in applause. These icons are not words but a code of images that symbolize ideas or emotions. They are easily reproduced and expressed in digital technology. There are a plethora of common emoji characters that are part of the text we type to communicate. When seen consciously, the graphic depictions can remain in the unconscious mind, like the Smiley Face. First posted in 1963, Smiley is an icon of the popular global culture whose simple expression of happiness and well-being can inspire a smile. Just close your eyes and visualize that cute generic grin. Imagine, a simple yellow circle with a funny face changed universal language. Smiley is often depicted blowing kisses, giving a wink, laughing with big teeth, frowning with tears, glowing with a halo, or wearing cool sunglasses. The icon gave rise to the contemporary emoticons that make our electronic messages so colorful and expressive.

The positive psychology of language makes it an important aspect of health. All language has a vibrational intention related to what we say and how we phrase it. Written or spoken, creative affirmations are positive words, messages, and phrases that articulate love, hopefulness, and a belief in positive potential. The language of love speaks and affirms with words, symbols, and gestures. Love is expressed with positive intention using creative affirmations that spiritually connect us to ourselves, others, and a higher power. Love and creativity are languages that exalt the mind-body-spirit and give meaning to life.

The nomenclature of love has positive resonance that speaks to who we are, and to who and what we care about. Through good and bad times, love is a peak creative experience. With empathic and affirming words, it endures eternally. The expression of love is essential to a good relationship and unconditional opening of the heart. All language has a vibrational intention related to what we say and how we express it. Language bears witness to our integrity, so the words that maintain a loving relationship must be the truth. Affirmations help us practice the positive articulation of our love and faith. One of the most beautiful phrases spoken with creative true voice is, "I love you." Love is expressed in phrases, conversations, letters, sentimental gestures, romantic messages, kind intentions, good deeds, and warm embraces. Love communicates, nurtures, and affirms.

One of the things I love about language is asking questions. What is your language creative wellness?

14: Sound Creative Wellness

hearing or feeling sound, mechanical wave energy, resonance, sound memory, rhythmic vibration, soundscapes, silence, sound nutrition, nature's song, vocal and instrumental music, music therapy, deep listening, spoken language, mantras

Sound is creative. A primordial sound birthed the Universe with a Big BANG! Sound is what we vibrationally hear and feel with the mind-body-spirit. It's a primary form of human sensation and communication. The phenomenon is a mechanical wave energy that is transmitted through air, water, and solids. We make sound vocally using breath and air flowing through body cavities in the mouth, nose or chest; or by causing a vibrational effect with any method or instrument to create noise.

Sound animates the life force with rhythm. It vibrationally *moves* energy. Resonance is the frequency at which an object or person vibrates. Sound resonates with our inner and outer harmony and disharmony. It nurtures and attunes our unique creative frequency. The vibrational energy transfers a change that creates a similar vibration. In an acoustic bio-musical sense, the concept of entrainment refers to synchronization of an organism in response to external rhythmic stimuli from another. Rhythm creates rhythm. Sound entices sound. Like inspires like. Going with the creative flow. Our brain responds to rhythmic vibration in ways that prompt humming and foot-tapping as we synchronize with the beat. Sound tracks through and all around us. The sensation calms or rouses in ways that balance energy. When creativity is in sync, the energy sounds and feels like two hearts beating as one, vibrationally entrained in a harmonious life-giving *motion*.

The human body is made of rhythmic sound. The breath enlivens, the heart beats, the voice speaks, the ears listen, the nose blows, the bowel growls, the 1-2, 1-2, 1-2 pace of our footsteps as we walk. Doctors listen for the sound of health inside the body with a stethoscope. We absorb sound from common sources and are immediately affected by it physically and psychologically. Sound nutrition is nurtured by habitat and what we are doing. There are positive and negative layers of sound that reflect our acoustic environment. The symphony of daily living includes background levels of white noise. The drone of a rotating fan, music playing as a car drives by, the rhythmic tick-tock clock, laughing voices nearby, or a windswept storm. These subtle sensations blend into our soundscape.

We each respond differently to sound and need a well-balanced vibrational diet that includes quiet and active experiences. Our responses are subjective. Sound that is calming to one person may be rousing to another, or vice versa. It is not good sound nutrition to be repeatedly exposed to loud frenetic noise which is linked to higher levels of stress, hypertension, heart disease, and hearing loss. Noise pollution is stressful, disorientating, and impairs hearing. Tinnitus is a common audiological and neurological condition that causes an acute or chronic ringing or buzzing in the ears. It is caused by various health factors and can be annoying and sometimes debilitating. Loud noise causes tinnitus and damages precious hearing, so it is best to turn down the headphones and use caution when it's noisy in a work or recreational environment.

Soundscapes set a mood that reflects what's happening at any moment. Life involves many kinds of sound. This requires us to edit and design our soundscapes, tuning in or tuning out. Experiencing calming, ambient sound can be challenging when living in a populated or discordant environment. Meditative sounds and music focus creativity in relaxing ways that insulate the senses from the hectic chorus of external noise. Total silence is a rare opportunity to conceive ideas born of reflection. There is resilience in silence. Practicing silence relieves stress, lowers blood pressure, and promotes sensory awareness. Mindfulness is a way to enjoy contemplative listening and what life sounds like in the moment. Elements of quiet are relative to our habitat and circumstances. Finding quietude can be challenging, especially when the chatter of the monkey-mind interrupts and distracts the calm. Sound is internal and external. Like any healthy diet, sound nutrition requires listening and living in balance.

Nature is never silent. Contemplative listening to natural sounds creates a sensory order in harmony with the body's innate rhythms. Like a vista of nature, we need the song of nature to align our senses with the Earth. There is no artificial equivalent for experiencing sounds in nature. The tones and vibrations are remarkably beautiful and diverse. The sound of a breeze rustling leaves, waves crashing along the shore, and birds singing in concert, are the organic audio that rekindles our connection to nature. Birds offer a harmonic symphony when we hear their memorable calls and communications that announce what's happening in nature. The sounds and songs of birds represent a unique natural language that inspires creative listening. The robin tweeting in springtime, wood thrush serenade in summer, farewell chorus of geese in autumn, and chirping chickadee-dee-dee-dee-dee in winter - birds remind us of the resplendence of nature's creative true voice. The loon's tremolo heard on a still lake, with the water amplifying the ancient bird's strangely beautiful call, is the healing sound of nature. The mechanical wave energy is more poignant as it travels across the liquid lake and is experienced by the human body, which is approximately 60% water, a medium that conducts sound. The sound of water *moving* and flowing is an element of nature that inspires creative wellness and a fluid connection to the rhythms of nature.

Vibrational medicine is an ancient healing medium. The premise is, when our life force is not in a harmonious flow, the physical body becomes diseased and disharmonious. The healing arts of Chinese medicine, acupuncture, and the Hindu chakra system all recognize the importance of vibrational energy meridians and pathways in the body. Color and sound stimulate the senses and health in similar ways. They have analogous wave frequencies and share a vibrational quality measured in the electromagnetic spectrum. Color is light. Sound converts into light and light into sound. Experiencing light and sound may be pleasing or unpleasant, depending on one's vibrational aesthetic. Methods of vibrational medicine involving light and sound therapies support a healthful energetic state as each cell and organ resonates with a balancing effect. This energy vibrates the spectrum of light and is the basis of chromotherapy.

In many cultures, sound and music are used for spiritual, ceremonial, and therapeutic purposes. Indigenous people use vibrational mediums to communicate, celebrate, and connect with the Earth's natural rhythms. The sounds of chant, song, musical instrument, and the human voice create healing effects. Traditional woodwind and percussion instruments for healing are handmade from natural materials, and have unique tonal qualities that open the listener to a state of well-being. Drums, rattles, whistles, flutes, zithers, bells, and chimes are played to support vibrational healing. The Tibetan singing bowls, Indonesian gamelan, and Australian didgeridoo are distinctive instruments known for inducing feelings of well-being that are commonly used in sound therapy. They are all harmonically dynamic. Especially the didgeridoo, which is a long wooden trumpet created by the aboriginal tribes of Australia. It makes an unforgettable prehistoric sound that can *move* the player and listener into an altered state. The tones are transformative, though an instrument doesn't need to be exotic to create healing vibrations. Piano, harp, violin, cello, saxophone, and guitar are classic instruments that create therapeutic sounds. The sound of any instrument creates wellness when played by a musician with healing intention,

From the cradle to the grave, music improves the quality of life. It has remarkable therapeutic effects on cognitive, physical, and emotional functions. Music therapy supports people when they are well or ill. Health-based applications involve music listening and making that provides wellness support and enjoyment. Direct methods of music stimulus can result in an immediate sense of sound wellness. It is measured by how a person feels and physical responses. In clinical and wellness settings, music therapy supports stress reduction, blood pressure, pain treatment, mental health, neurodegenerative disorders, stroke recovery, memory enhancement, and general patient wellness. Music therapy is a vibrational remedy that calms or rouses the senses and activates the healing qualities of the life force energy. The power of music to heal the human condition is a miracle and a mystery.

Music is multi-sensory. We feel music because it touches all the senses. We hear sound with the entire body and vibrationally embody it in response to our environment. This is the way an artist makes *moving* music. An example of how sound is experienced by the body is the story of Helen Keller

(1880-1968), a deaf-blind, American writer and activist. She overcame her communication disabilities to become an internationally famous speaker and author who advocated for women's rights and various social causes in her time. As an older woman, she visited Martha Graham (1894-1990), the preeminent modern dancer and choreographer, at her legendary New York dance studio. Without touching them, Martha encouraged Helen to use her body to experience the *movement* of the dancers who performed, and her hands to feel the sound of the accompanying instruments and vocalist. She felt the rhythm and sound in the air and reacted to it with spontaneous dance. The mechanical waves in sound are how a deaf person may feel the rhythmic vibrations of music or how a blind person may feel color.

The prolific German composer Ludwig Van Beethoven (1770-1827) was deaf most of his life, however, he had a genius for feeling his music. The classical artist used numeric patterns and melodic structures in his compositions that relate to mathematics. Math + *movement* + emotion = music! He didn't have a good ear, but he was a good counter and feeler of the beat who eloquently built his musical masterworks with elements of arithmetic, rhythmic patterns, harmonic dissonance, perceived tone, and pure emotion. Beethoven used musical motifs with three short notes and one long note in his famous *5th Symphony*, which is perhaps the most recognized in the history of music. "*da, da, da, daah…da, da, da, daah*". Ludwig was a deaf musician who could hear with all the senses.

These are elements of music: RHYTHM - *the sound of breath and time*; MELODY - *the sound of emotion and meaning*; REPETITION - *the sound of the familiar and knowable*; BASE - *the sound of deep roots and strength*; and HARMONY - *the sound of peace and connectedness*. Music is a portal for listening and responding with the mind-body-spirit. This sensory medium is most like our own energy. The effects of music are immediate and lasting. Our instincts respond to the vibrational qualities of music in ways that energize vitality and imprint the psyche. How music makes us heal and feel is relative to personal interpretation as the maker or listener. Different melodies and rhythms evoke different responses, and we all have musical preferences.

Listening to favorite music is a peak creative experience, the soundtrack of life. For me, the physical experience of hearing and feeling music transports my spirit and opens my heart with rapture. It allows me to embody my vibrational energy and can bring me to tears, stir deep feelings, and inspire my best creative works. Probably you have a favorite musical work that *moves* you in a special way. Can you hear it in your creative memory right now? Music holds a feeling and a time. When music speaks to me, I am able to recall it in my audio imagination like a mental radio. Our muscles and organs have a physical memory of all the energy they possess. Sound energy can fill a space and a memory. The mystical quality of sound affects our vibrational energy with the gift of being able to creatively recall a thought of music or sound and it is heard in the conscious mind. Vibrational memory lives within us and is one of the last sensory abilities to leave the body at death. Music is experiential. It imprints memory and time. The oldies-but-goodies quality of remembering music makes it a positive factor in longevity. This is why music is recognized as one of the most effective therapeutic methods for helping dementia patients find an oasis of memory.

Listening to music, playing a musical instrument, and singing all prime the brain for higher executive functioning. These activities build math and language skills, improve memory and physical coordination, promote confidence, and provide entertainment. Through music, we express individualism and communicate values. Music is a medium for feeling and responding to empathy that invokes deep, active listening and an ability to attune ourselves to the meaning and physical sensation of the medium. Music listening and performing is part of every culture. It is a universal language that connects us to each other like no other art form. Music informs, entertains, educates, and expresses the creative true voice of humanity with every note and beat. Everyone needs music, every day.

Words are the sounds of language. When set to music, they are a powerful form of creative communication. The human voice is truly expressed when singing or speaking. A tender love ballad or uplifting anthem, songs give a lyric shape to sound with melismatic vocal phrases, dulcet tones, and rhythmic tempos. We tend to remember words set to music and it is often easier to recall song lyrics than lines of poetry. Sung or spoken, the power and beauty of poetry requires us to be present with the words in the linguistic moment. It is why the sound of a poem read aloud, especially when performed by the poet, is profoundly experienced. The rhythmic sound of words creatively engages and expands active listening. This deep audio attention opens sensory awareness and our deep thinking and feeling. Words broadcast who we are and what we know and feel. They ask and answer questions and relate the meaning of life. Words make up everyday language and are the common sounds all humans share.

The musical sound of language rhythmically vibrates in the text of popular books written by Dr. Seuss. His upbeat style of poetic alliteration, assonance, and onomatopoeia is memorable in the sound lexicon of American children's literature. Theodore Seuss Geisel (1904-1990), a.k.a. Dr. Seuss, was a marvelous illustrator and poet whose books represent some of the greatest kid's rap on the planet. The charming syncopated sounds of his words are remembered and repeated. The first books I could read were *One Fish, Two Fish, Red Fish, Blue Fish* and *The Cat in the Hat*. I was able to read and remember the words because of the repetitive rhythmic text. My early sense of sound guided me into a learning experience and those great pictures! Sound is a way to learn and *Oh, The Places You'll Go!* ..."You have brains in your head. You have feet in your shoes. You can steer yourself any direction you choose. You're on your own. And you know what you know. And YOU are the guy who'll decide where to go." Poetic words of wisdom from Dr. Seuss.

Through sound communication and awareness, we experience some of life's most creative moments. The senses are crystalline and enlivened. The vibrational quality of sound touches emotions and imprints itself in our consciousness and unconsciousness. Listening trains the ear to hear and interpret and respond appropriately. We listen with the mind and heart. We listen to learn and be present with the sound of music playing or a person speaking. It's important to listen and be heard. The sounds we hear resonate with intention. Hearing a kind and reassuring voice is far better sound nutrition than negativity, criticism, or nothing. The sounds of words can nurture or neglect creativity. Vocal affirmations are essential in any relationship. These are positive words, said to ourselves or others, and the words others say to us. They are the mantras we say and repeat with good intentions. Saying and hearing healthy words that are meaningful and supportive sounds like - *You can do it! Great work, well done. Keep the faith. I am creative. I love you.*

The tone and intention of spoken words engender positive healing effects that can last a lifetime. There is a phenomenon of sound, both musical vibrations and sung or spoken words, that allows our memory to recall it like a mental radio. It holds a space and a time. We hear the sound in absence of its source. The creative recall of particular sounds reverberates in our hearts. Many years after my mother's death, my memory can still hear the sound of her affirming voice saying, "Laura Anna, you are a child of my spirit." Mom, thanks for those words. This one is for you.

With breath and voice, we create sounds that echo the dynamics of the Universe. We use our breath to make sound. Breathing supports both vocal capacity and overall health. For creative true voice to be clear and sustained, we need breath to fill our vessel with sound. There are chords of sound that connect the mind-body-spirit when created with breath. "OM" is a Sanskrit intonation that represents the basic sound of everything, containing all other sounds. This sacred mantra attunes us to the universal cosmic vibration. OM is chanted from the back of the throat to the front and then out through the lips. The vibrational repetition of the practice creates harmony, peace, and bliss for the chanter and all who hear and feel its sound. It's a good vibration that makes more good vibrations. Amazing, the positive energy of creating a single sound connects us with the essence of all things. "OM," said the Universe.

What is your sound creative wellness?

15: Visual Creative Wellness

look to see to remember to enjoy, observation, point of view, brain-eyes-hands function, making or seeing visual art, drawing, painting, photography, video, chromotherapy, color, light, rainbow code, internal or external imagery, creative visualization

Creativity is visual. Looking and seeing is how we observe life. The eyes see images in our external view. The mind's eye sees internal images. Visual creativity is our aesthetic sensibility. Blind or sighted, it's what the imagination looks like. Humans self-express and communicate with varying degrees of visual literacy. This involves communication skills and the ability to interpret what we see and imagine. We use visual literacy when sketching, reading, writing, gesturing, crafting, making, and pondering.

Internal and external imagery informs visual language. Instinctively, we communicate visually and make our mark or match. Inspired by internal imagery, we make a visual mark to establish our original ideas and existence. Inspired by external imagery, we make a visual match to interpret what we observe and experience. A painter creates what they imagine, making their mark, or documents what's in their visual field, matching what is seen. The creative process is both internal and external, abstract and realistic, *moving* and changing, depending on artistic interpretation. Our visual perception is how we see things and express an aesthetic point of view.

Sight tends to be a dominant creative sense. The way we see personalizes how we process visual information. The eyes are like open windows to sensory awareness. Being a visual artist and writing this essay has helped me understand that my process for creating language is as visual as making a painting. Words create pictures. As I contemplated the subject, being a sighted person, I tried to relate what it is like to be visually impaired. Blind since birth, the brilliant American singer and songwriter Stevie Wonder (1950-) became a metaphor for trying to imagine the mind's remarkable capacity to create visual language. Truly a wonder, when Stevie sings it, one can rhythmically see and feel the higher ground. His musical lyrics are highly visual and tell stories in the key of life in harmony with what he sees and feels in his heart and soul. When Stevie Wonder's hands meet his harmonica or keyboard, he expresses his creative true voice with mind-body-spirit and all the senses.

The power of the creative mind's eye can transcend an optic disability because we see intuitively with all the senses. Sight is stimulated by sound, touch, smell, taste, and insight. Visual capacities activate creativity, whether sighted or blind. The visual languages of tactile signing and braille, and virtually everything they touch, allows a blind person to use their hands to communicate and get information in a 3-dimensional form. The brain, eyes, and hands flow and function together to create a visual language, even when eyesight is impaired.

I learned how this capacity is possible while teaching a community origami program at a local library. A woman in her mid-seventies came to the event to learn how to fold a paper crane. I taught her and others in a group to make the iconic form by demonstrating the folds as I lead the origami process with my voice instruction. Once everyone in the group had made their first crane, the woman announced to me that she was legally blind. She could barely see the graphic pattern on the origami paper, yet, her agile and sensitive fingers felt the edges as she mindfully creased the folds. Watching how this tactile process helped the woman transcend a visual disability, and hearing her talk gleefully about her artistic accomplishment, has deepened my understanding of the power of art to heal. The eyes and mind's eye helps the hands and brain make creativity happen.

We witness the world around us by paying attention and observing it. Curiosity and wonder are *motivators* for perceiving and interpreting what we see. The act of seeing involves our ability to recognize, remember, and relate images. Active looking changes the way we view the world and ourselves. To be present and really LOOK, we observe what is seen and not seen. "Look to see to remember to enjoy." This was what my most-loved art teacher would say to us in every class. When looking at the world from our point of view - the pencil on a table, the person on a train, the colors in an evening sky - we can be in the moment, in time and space, with the simple and strange beauty around us.

Looking can make us want to copy what we see and generate a new form of the original. Copying and documenting are ways that we learn, model ideas, and acquire information. Observing engenders intellectual inquiry. We ask questions and look for answers until we see them. This is the way of the artist-scientist, the brain-eyes-hands physics of creativity. The process is a balanced brain function. The right brain hemisphere produces the bulk of creative expression, while the left simultaneously makes key contributions that facilitate the activity. We are aware and respond. What we see *moves* the brain to *move* the hands. Visual creativity connects the brain, eyes, and hands to perform expressive tasks. The physical *movement* of the human eye functioning in all directions stimulates the visually curious brain to inquire, innovate, and give creative ideas a physical form with our hands.

Visual artists know the foundation of art is to observe the internal and external imagery we see and create a response using any media. Making visual art improves motor skills, dexterity, and critical thinking. It gives form to our thoughts and feelings. Like all visual and performing arts, drawing enhances perception and learning, develops new skills, and builds on natural talents. Drawing is the basic structure for making visual art or illustrating an idea. The impulse to draw is instinctual. Children draw before they learn to write or read, and love to make their mark on all sorts of things. Drawing is a primary visual language and fundamental way we relate information.

Until recent decades, basic drawing was taught in most school curriculums as a way to learn by observation. Before photos or video, we recorded what was seen by making a rendering and understanding something by really looking at it. The subject could be a person, place, thing, or idea. Drawing has educational value for every student. The skill enriches many creative professions. As global education priorities shift from STEM to STEAM - science, technology, engineering, **art**, and math will become the new paradigm for student achievement and innovation. Schools improve the quality of education, at all grade levels, when they support the arts and reinstate drawing and studio arts programs.

Like handwriting, drawing activates the brain-eyes-hands function. It is a balanced brain activity that engenders personal awareness and learning. We observe and draw from life, memory, the mind's eye, and from the well within. We sketch out our ideas and make a drawing before we make it. Drawing styles can be detailed and meditative, loose and animated, and are as individualistic as we are. Sometimes working on a large scale drawing can be a catharsis of physical energy, and focusing on a smaller work more calming and mindful. Coloring with crayons or colored pencils is often our first drawing lesson. It is no coincidence that adult coloring books are a popular trend because they are an inexpensive and immediate medium for creative wellness. This simple and enjoyable form of creative self-care is relaxing and meditative. Coloring, doodling, and sketching are liberating ways to let the mind draw that provides the therapeutic benefit of just letting go and seeing what happens.

Anyone who likes to draw knows the mindfulness of observational sketching. The way to learn to draw is by drawing. There are no rules, just the brain, eyes, and hands free to work in unison with a preferred medium. The rule of thumb is the more you draw, the better you will draw. It is a nonlinear process because what we observe is multidimensional. There are basic principles and techniques that can be applied to refine skills, like how to render using perspective or drawing a figure in proportion. When I teach drawing, I instruct students to let their eyes and mind lead their hand and feel the image in an intuitive way, to see with all the senses. To see and be art, not just to look at something, but to feel it. To see things feelingly, makes good art and a good life.

This also applies to painting and understanding the fluidity of color. The way to learn to paint is by painting. Get the medium in your hands. See and feel the process. Painting is my favorite visual art medium, and whether using watercolors or acrylics, there is a natural flow in brushstrokes that integrates color and form. The process of painting involves the phenomena of color and light. Painters are lifetime students of color and light who must work continuously to master their medium.

My painter's eye and heart are inspired by nature, both the natural environment and human nature. I paint for personal meditation, aesthetic exploration, and to create a visual work that is meaningful and healing. It is my mind-body-spirit practice and peak creative experience. If you'd like to start or restart a painting practice, I recommend a simple set of watercolors, a wash brush, a few sheets of watercolor paper, cup of water, and SEE what happens. Painting is playful discovery. Try any fluid medium that **art**iculates your expression.

Visual art trains the eyes and hands to see and express value, line, form, shape, texture, motion, proportion, perspective, light, and color. Making or viewing visual art is an opportunity to see. Our visual field engenders two-dimensional and three-dimensional art. 2-D art is a flat work like a painting, drawing, or photograph. 3-D art is viewed from multiple perspectives like sculpture, ceramics, or assemblage. Abstractly, I can relate, from my own process, that creating a 2-D painting can feel like I'm 3-D sculpting with color and form, though the image is flat. Sometimes my HB pencil feels like clay. Making or viewing art is a multidimensional experience that stimulates sensory activity on many levels. The basic elements of art and principles of design are guides for visual observation and rendering a technique. Mostly, it's the artist's perception and interpretation that makes it a work of visual art.

Photography is an enjoyable way to cultivate the art of observation. It is one of the most important art forms of modern times with the ability to tell a story and history in a single frame in real-time. A rich medium to explore, photography combines artistry, point of view, and technical skill. A good photographer knows how to work with the light and subject. They see and capture an image that inspires the viewer to see. The medium requires the artist to be out in the world, in a moment and place, and to record a visual story. The world is full of visual experience, created and observed. We can take pictures and video on our phones, anytime and anywhere. These are the selfies and snapshots of life. Using social media, we can develop an optical platform by what we photograph, post, or pin to our profile. Digital cameras see the world in a new light. This popular and portable method captures how we picture life and is creating a new visual language that is immediate, inclusive, and accessible. Visual art, combined with technology, is a powerful medium for expressing creative true voice. By sharing information and imagery, we are able to see the world. As a population of citizen artists, seeing together informs, unites, and expands collective empathy.

Visual creativity provides opportunities to see and express, to make our mark or match, and to art-make, art-take, and art-give. The shutterbug, movie fan, flower gardener, puzzle builder, interior decorator, greeting card maker, fashionista, graphic doodler, gallery goer, home crafter, and cake baker. Every creator can enjoy the benefits of visual creative wellness just by doing what comes naturally. Visual expression is intrinsic to human nature and driven by our interests and a desire to do loved creative things. Like sound, we need good visual nutrition. This includes a pleasing environment with color and light, vistas of nature and beauty, inspiring places and spaces, and seeing the familiar things and people in our lives. Visual health involves the multidimensional eyes seeing organically in the 3-D real world. This means limiting the time spent looking at the unreal world on a flat digital screen. Visual creative wellness is how and what we see, and the experience of our internal and external imagery.

At all stages of life, visual creativity supports health and longevity. The American folk painter, Grandma Moses (1860-1961) lived until she was 101 years old, and didn't start painting until she was in her seventies, which she took up only after arthritis made her embroidery too painful. Grandma Moses did well with her therapeutic choice of painting. She created iconic images of rural American traditions that are cultural treasures. Her classic works became a phenomenon in the 1950s. Nationally, her charming art was in museums and she licensed designs to make a branded collection of printed fabric, dinnerware, and lifestyle items that were commercially popular. Anna Mary Robertson Moses was a visual influencer, entrepreneur, and spirited woman who inspired people of all ages with her naive style of art. She painted her real life in a real style. For those who may yet consider picking up a paintbrush, know that age and ailment can be transcended on canvas, and that no experience is required.

You don't have to be a painter or see a painting to experience the benefits of color and light. It's the primary way we perceive the world that informs the senses. Color is a physical phenomenon of light. Visible light is a form of energy. The visible part of the electromagnetic spectrum is the color we see. Sound and light share similar mechanical wave energies and are both visible as color. Light converts into sound, and sound into light. Color is the vibrational light energy we can see and feel. Red, orange, yellow, green, blue, indigo and violet are the seven consistent colors seen when light is refracted through a reflective medium. ROY G BIV is an acronym for the order in which the colors appear. The consistency of the spectrum is related to the electromagnetic field and vibration of the energy wavelengths that make up color. Red vibrates at the lowest speed on the spectrum, indigo vibrates at the highest. Black is the absence of light. All the spectrum colors combined create white, scientifically, though a painter's palette may have a different interpretation. I imagine, that if a painter could mix colors with pure light, not opaque white, then white would look translucent, like light reflecting on water. My painter's eye tries to see and understand the colors that make up the bright reflections of natural light on water. With focused observation, I can see that each sparkle of white light reflects the visible spectrum of colors. Every drop, every photon of water is a rainbow. The surface of a lake shimmering in the light mirrors how space *moves* in ripples from gravity, wind, and heat. Color is energy in *motion*. The radiant luminance of water in natural light, with all the colors reflecting the sky and land, is a visual image that humbles most landscape painters. Color and light are essential to enlivening art and life.

We perceive color biologically, environmentally, psychologically, and culturally. Each of us relates differently to tones, hues, shades, and values. Even a person who is colorblind can interpret different values of light. Like sound, since ancient times, the vibrational and psychophysical qualities of color have been investigated by scientists, artists, and healers. Seeing color triggers responses in the brain. We can visualize it in the creative mind's eye. Theories about color and its effects on the body are based on the fundamental principles of organic science and how we perceive color. Chromotherapy has roots in Chinese and Ayurvedic medicine and the Native American medicine wheel, which has five healing elements represented by the colors yellow, red, blue, black, and green. The German artist-scientist Johann Wolfgang von Goethe (1749-1832) wrote in his book, *Theory of Colors*, about the physiological effects of color, which seventy-five years later influenced the more philosophical investigations of Rudolf Steiner (1861-1925), an Austrian who connected color to science and spiritualism. Goethe's observations of the contrasting effects of colors led him to a detailed arrangement of the *Color Wheel*, a model that defines primary, secondary, and tertiary colors.

During the nineteenth century, color theory in America evolved in practice through the work of Edwin Babbitt. He used chromotherapy to treat physical and emotional aliments with the fundamentals of thermal, electrical, and neutral colors. Babbitt worked therapeutically with colored glass lenses that were activated by light. He would apply his theories by using specially tinted lenses to activate color-charged water as a health elixir, which resulted in well-documented cures of common illnesses. Babbitt believed in the wellness benefits of natural light. He installed colorful chromolumes in treatment rooms at his Victorian clinic and prescribed colored glass for well care in the home. A natural healer, Babbitt believed that thermal colors (red, orange, yellow) excite or raise blood pressure; electric colors (blue, indigo, violet) calm or reduce blood pressure; and the neutral color green has a stabilizing effect on the entire human system. Neuroscience links green to creative *motivation* and stress reduction. Green is the fourth and median color in the spectrum. It is the neutral balance of warm (red, orange, yellow) and cool (blue, indigo, violet) palettes. Color affects how we think and feel, and it offers wonderful creative possibilities for restoring health and vitality. If we visualize our human body as light, then all the colors vibrating and blending together would be a rainbow, the aura of homeostasis.

Color naturally stimulates creativity. We perceive color emotionally and physically through the senses. We have only to look at the spectrum in nature to see how color sustains life. Nature artfully uses visible color and form to create biodiversity. Plants are colored and shaped to attract pollinators. Visual color provides essential camouflage in a habitat and sends messages within a species. Affected by light, colors change with circadian rhythms throughout the seasons. Nature imprints life with a rainbow code. Every living thing has its own combination of colors that visually forms its existence. Creatures of nature, we each have a rainbow code that articulates who we are and how we survive and thrive. Your rainbow code is how you personally and creatively live with color, what you wear, the environments you occupy, your possessions, and the food you eat. Your rainbow code can have colors arranged in any palette that promotes tonal happiness and wellness. Because life is an artwork in progress, I'm always evolving my rainbow code. My color palette reflects the brightly colored artworks on my studio walls, and is evident in the collection of eclectic fashion accessories and curios that share my space, all blending together in my unique spectrum. Loud or muted, bright or pastel, black or white, your rainbow code shows your true colors. A universal visual language, color is emotive and expressive. In our shared culture, the rainbow code identifies beliefs and interests, simply by wearing the colors symbolically associated with what *motivates* us. It can be the color of a favorite sports team, political party, or an important cause we support. People wear awareness ribbons and t-shirts in colors that recognize a health or social interest. This creates a visual placebo with positive effect. Color activism for a cause can be a powerful symbol.

All that we see and perceive, all the colors and light, shapes and forms in all variations and perspectives, comprise our internal and external imagery. It is what we envision and view every day. Creative visualization is a method for seeing life, what it is, and what we imagine it can be. Self-guided imagery and creative visualization are ways to observe and balance the mind-body-spirit. We can create a representation of wellness by creating positive visuals that help focus energy. It is subjective imagery that represents what we think and feel, need and desire. A visual affirmation is a sign of faith or a picture of our dream. It can be part of a personal altar or a special view that reminds us of our purpose and passion. Creative visualizations are inspired by art, photographs, words, symbols, colors, objects, or artifacts of nature. This is our personal picture library. The power of positive intention and hope for all things good in life is represented by what and how we see the world.

Use creative visualization to create your best life. When you "see" your life as creative, it opens the flow of expressive experience. Having a visual of creativity *moves* energy and intention to manifest what we envision into an experience. Take a moment for this creative visualization. What does your creativity look like? What are you doing when you say, *I am creative*? Can you see the things you need and desire? Who and what shows up to be your co-creators? How do you visualize a peak creative experience? Look to SEE your creativity and remember to enjoy it every day.

What is your visual creative wellness?

Part Three: Doing Creativity

16: Creative Flow

Where is the source of human creativity? Look inward to self, it is there. Look outward to the Universe, it is there. As it is within, so without. The creative source is a singular and collective continuum that is interconnected to the innermost parts of our being and outermost parts of the cosmos. It is the life force energy that is above, below, and all around us, flowing through and beyond our human form. It comes from all that was, is, and will be. Creativity is a natural rhythm that energetically makes order or chaos with varying degrees of change. A balance is achieved as creative energy is generated and regenerated.

The creative source is the center of ourselves and everything, where purpose and passion are enlivened and expressed. It is a portal of potential that contains shadow and light, what is known and unknown. A force for good, it's alive with the vitality of energy in *motion.* It is the catalyst for change that creates and re-creates, and awakens new ways of creative thinking, doing, and being.

Though mysterious, the creative source is not alien or different in substance. It is not a muse that appears separate from ourselves. It is a part of our nature, not apart. Creativity is a change in energy, a cause seeking effect. Change is the one constant of energy and life. Physicists and gurus know energy can't be destroyed. It is active, *moving,* and changing in some form. This is the eternal fountain from which creativity springs. Like the metaphor, it is the pebble, and the still and *moving* water, and all that is affected by the energetic flow. The pebble is the inspiration, the idea, the thing, the change, the purpose. It is a force that transforms energy, changing the water within time and space. The water is the flow of creativity *moving* in gravitational waves. It is the vital substance and eternal wellspring of wellness, the conscious and unconscious ebb and flow of thoughts and feelings. It is the passion, the thirst for life that fills and empties the grail within.

The creative source is in every living thing. It is the who, what, when, where, why, and how of creativity. This native confidence to create impels us to self-actualize and self-express using instinct and skill. It activates the mediumistic qualities of the mind-body-spirit. We all possess a medial quality that opens sentient awareness and an aesthetic observation of internal and external experience. This is a conscious presence of the unconscious when we have a foothold in both the physical and metaphysical worlds. The imagination lingers in this zone where the veil is thin and perception heightened. Here is the natural source of creativity, the spring that bubbles up where we drink and become refreshed, inspired and in spirit. It is a fluid and flowing force that enlivens, an oscillating, ever-changing *movement* of pure energy. It is the pulse and impulse of life.

Our sentient creative nature responds to any environment activated by the senses. This is a conscious and unconscious observation involving sight, sound, touch, smell, and taste. It influences how we think and feel, and initiates *movement*. Our intuition involves all the senses and is the gateway of inspiration. Creativity is a response to sensory capacities. Seeing a colorful sunset, hearing a favorite song, feeling the softness of yarn, smelling a box of crayons, or tasting fresh garden herbs. Our highly attuned senses permeate how we communicate and get information, and imprints our perception with active creative experience and active memory of it.

The flow of creative energy is a phenomenon described by artists, musicians, writers, athletes, scientists, psychologists, philosophers, lovers, and gurus since ancient times. It's the addicting part of doing creativity because flow feels so good and opens an expanded state of awareness that frees the mind-body-spirit. It often feels like an uncontrolled force, but where it goes is wonderful. Flow is a direct conduit for energy to follow intention that is activated before, during, and after creative practice. Go with this flow. When there is a need and desire to create, the life force responds in harmony with energetic intention. The process absorbs and engages. Guided by intention, we can change to adapt and learn, inventing and reinventing as we go. Flow is a natural high when we are not distracted and definitely not bored. We lose a sense of time and find ourselves by getting lost. When a creative practice has full attention and intention, it feels amazing. 100% engagement when doing a loved creative thing is a good thing.

Creative flow is an organic process that is not about push and control. It is not an external force. We each have a unique channel for tapping the flow. Spontaneous and uninhibited, the sensation feels like a pathway to liberation through the senses. It is creativity in action, self-directed and self-aware. We are free to engage while being detached. The feel-good state of flow is an organic proclivity that is naturally enlivening. We are happy and things are *moving* well which fills our well with wellness. Flow is a way of being balanced and present in response to experience, a way of giving and receiving. The body follows the mind that is following the spirit. There is a glow to flow. Creativity flowing feels like falling in love, a free fall into the mystery where you follow your heart. It's a deep connection that just feels right and safe. This is the realm of unconditional trust, which is powerfully healing in any relationship.

Creative flow is fluid. It instinctually *moves* to make a change and evolves to create something original that makes life better and more beautiful. This fluidity is the vehicle that transforms energy. The singular feeling is exhilarating and strengthening. It is a peak creative experience that connects us to our higher power and purpose when we are living our passion. Flow is a different state of well-being and deep contentment that feels authentic. It is an embodiment and immersion in the essence of our being.

Flow is the divine gravity that pulls a raindrop to Earth, and into the stream, where it drifts down the river to the sea's tidal surf. Creative flow propels us like water, *moving* and going with the energy of our creative intention. To find balance, we need to be like water, and to become flexible and able to adapt to elements that impact the experience. Sometimes, when trying to concentrate and open up to creative expression, negative thoughts and anxiety can steal focus. TRUST, and keep going. The pebble is hard, solid, and inert until it is *moved* by the soft, fluid, flowing water. The water smooths and transforms what is rough and stagnant. It frees what is restrained. Be like the flow of water.

The visceral moment of expression is an act of drawing in, like a life-giving breath, that inspires the outward release of our creative flourishing. It is natural and necessary, just like breathing. Pure moments of inspiration are free of restraints that liberate the creative mind. This unfiltered freedom allows for abstract thinking. Intellect and intuition *move* the imagination and creativity begins. Need, desire, and curiosity direct the flow of expression. The mind's eye imagines and an image comes into awareness.

Inspiration invites us to muse, ponder, incubate, innovate, invent, wonder, dream, discover, compose, make, and let our guiding genius practice original play. Inspiration is like a pop! It is a playful release of spirited expression that is spontaneous and edifying. Inspiration is the aha! insight that activates our creative thinking (mind), doing (body), and being (spirit). The tingling sensation is an awareness that transcends the ordinary and feels like a new beginning. This is the genesis of a peak creative experience.

The great flowing river of creativity *moves* through the mind-body-spirit in powerful trickles and gentle floods. We recognize inspiration in colorful brushstrokes, poetic music, great inventions, actions that change the world, unconditional love, and the common things that make us uniquely human. What is this brilliant sensation? Is it the spirit expressed? Inspiration is an animated impulse that comes from both a need and desire to express thoughts and feelings. We are inspired by need because it is the mother of invention, and by desire because love and hope illuminate the human spirit.

The call of creativity is heard with all the senses and felt with the heart. Because we love, we hear the call and are inspired to create. This call and response is the creative libido naturally manifesting our purpose and passion. When we live with an open heart, our daily existence is naturally creative because it is nurtured by a desire to love and care for ourselves, others, and the greater good. Creativity nurtures love, and love nurtures creativity. These parallel flowing energies are co-creators. Our creative nature has the psyche of a lover that needs and passionately desires the sensual embrace of sensory expression.

Inspiration comes when we explore an idea or interest or are influenced by the aesthetic of an individual or group. Traveling and experiencing different places and cultures expands creativity and cultivates diversity. The people we meet throughout life's journey are our most treasured and abundant sources of inspiration. Spending time with a friend can be one of the best creative *motivators*. Peers, teachers, and mentors encourage ideas for expression and offer insights for developing our unique skills and gifts. The well is forever full and flowing when we draw from the reserve of those special people who have inspired our lives.

Inspiration happens in a flash or over a lifetime. A big inspiration can become an arch of ideas, connected by a strong intellectual foundation that gives it balance and brilliance. An inspired idea can be seeded in the psyche in youth and stay with us until we become our inspiration. The value of jotting down a novel thought as it occurs is that it could blossom into a future brilliant project. Our entire life memory and the collective incubation of our thoughts and feelings are the seeds of inspiration that grow into new experiences. These seeds are cultivated in the mind's garden amid the quiet and noise of life's everyday compost, sometimes for many growing seasons.

What inspires you? How inspiration happens is unique to each of us. The things we like or dislike often spark creativity. Transformative or everyday events, and a broad range of internal and external factors can start the process. Creativity is inspired by difficult situations, the need to manage stress or illness, or basic problem-solving. In balance, it happens when enjoying a friendship, engaging in a favorite hobby, or learning a new skill. Often brilliant insights come when we break old habits and embrace new experiences, and at exciting thresholds when we are uninhibited and dare to take risks to reinvent convention. Inspiration manifests in dreams, prayers, meditation, and self-reflection. It seemingly appears in the mist or is simply shining in plain sight. We are inspired by what we believe.

Be inspired. Nurture ideas - make a sketch, take a picture, write it down, sing it out, live the moment. Flow seeks a departure, a journey to an unknown place that is known only upon arrival. Flow begins with the trickles and floods of energy released by the enlivened creative source. *FULL FLOW* feels oceanic and excites the soul. It's up to you to take a risk and take the adventure, float in the calm and swim hard upstream, propel upward into the light and dive downward into the shadows, and open the senses to let the imagination run free. In the river of creativity, *MOVE!* Let go. Do not hold on to the shore. Swim in the fertile middle. TRUST that the river's destination is the way to wellness and transforming your life. Enjoy and celebrate this freedom and go with the creative flow.

17: Creative People

The way we perceive and present ourselves in the world is animated by our purpose, passion, and creative individualism. Creativity is an essential life skill and our most renewable and valuable natural resource. We are creative people in our personal and professional lives, and local and global communities. We initiate to make our mark, or imitate to make our match. We are creative people who originate and innovate in beautiful and practical ways that make life better. What drives this remarkable quality? From ancient to modern times, the fields of neuroscience, psychology, sociology, anthropology, and the arts and humanities have tried to answer this question. Overall, the diverse data and collective wisdom defines human creativity as a universal quality and positive phenomenon that evolves our species and makes us happier and healthier people.

The art of science tries to understand and define the creative mind. Scientists provide empirical facts, and artists give them meaning. Creativity defies the confines of data. The results will always be flawed because it's an organic response that is original, sometimes planned, and often random. It is a multidimensional process informed by internal and external factors. Beyond science, our perception of the experience is the realm of magic and mystery and can't be explained.

Our expressive styles are innate or acquired. Everyone's creative normal is different. Universal aspects of creativity include cognitive disinhibition and the ability to embrace new ideas and experiences, divergent and independent thinking, being open to sensory stimuli, acting on inspiration, and persistence to create something original. These are key indicators of creative engagement and achievement.

The creative mind works to understand and sustain what it needs and desires by organically synthesizing information and experience. Curiosity and wonder *motivate* learning. Creative people want to learn about the world and things. We are wizards of metaphorical thinking who like to experiment and test theories. We are seers and doers. Instincts and interests inform our craft. This positive growth mindset is not stagnant. Creative people *move* on ideas and act to create. It is how we evolve and better our life condition. We are brilliant when we break old habits and try new things, get out of the box and out of our way. Creativity is liberating. When this inborn power is in *motion*, it opens sensory awareness to expression, freeing our native confidence to create.

Creative people are active lookers who observe everything and view life as an opportunity for self-expression. We are *motivated*, self-directed learners compelled to daydream and incubate ideas and are often autodidacts with the self-discipline to work independently. A creative person imagines then knows how to organize and do the work required to create it. Many creatives are polymaths with broad interests and are well-informed and highly skilled in varied fields. The hallmarks of a creative person are the resilience to persevere and direct focus, even when confronted with skepticism, resistance, or failure, and the courage to take risks and pursue an idea or belief. These qualities, and the ability to connect concepts and create new ones, and embrace diversity and examine life in different ways, are what transforms humanity and advances civilization.

People are everyday creative. We are artisans of life. Some people self-identify as "artists" and spend their lives working in an artistic discipline or intellectual domain. It includes visual artists, musicians, writers, actors, performers, crafters, designers, makers, and healers, but is not limited to these vocations. Often, the impulse comes early in life with an awareness that you are perceiving the world and can feel the visceral response to create. I remember being very young and looking at my hand, thinking that I was the smallest person I knew, so this must be the smallest hand in the world. It was a beautiful spring day as I was sitting on a green hillside. I looked up at the big blue sky to see its expansiveness. Where did it go, and how far? I put my hand up and looked at it in comparison to the sky, first at an arm's length, then pulling my hand toward my face. Close to my eyes, the proportion of my small hand from that point of view was quite large compared to the vast landscape of the sky. I was curious about this perspective and my relationship to it. I wanted to grab a piece of that blue and what was beyond.

Artists are highly active lookers and observers. We seek expression and a way of understanding our inner and outer world. The artist knows about process; how to let inspiration guide imagination, incubate an idea, prepare and make it, and to create something that expresses creative true voice. The inclination to create can be driven by a *motivational* intensity that transcends the average need to self-actualize, amplified by a strong desire to self-express. An artist can be an introvert or extrovert. They may be viewed as being provocative, eccentric, or outspoken. They dare to reveal a truth that others cannot accept. Creating shock of the new and different is the unconventional way for some artists, while others illustrate artifacts of the past, and the bravest reinvent convention with a vision for the future. The artist creates what yearns to be born. Always of their time, and sometimes before and beyond, artists define the zeitgeist, the spirit of the times.

There are unfortunate stereotypes of "the artist" being a pariah, a black sheep on the fringe of their community who is stigmatized by the notion that creative people are unstable and suffer angst. In fact, psychology studies show the act of creativity is associated with positive emotions, resiliency, and growth. Angst can be related to a degree of tension that makes good art, requiring the creator to work hard to make a singular expression. This can sometimes be coupled with waves of self-doubt and emotional or erratic behavior, which is not required to make good art, though it may drive the making of great art. The isolation of otherness can be part of a singular nature to work toward a goal or vision that lives big within the psyche. It takes many, many thousands of hours to achieve mastery.

The link between depression and hyper-creative people was recognized by the ancient Greeks. There is scientific research linking creativity with depression, because extreme behavior and mental illness have impacted some of the most creative and visionary people in history. Likely, there are a larger number of people who suffer from psychological problems because they don't express their creativity. Depression and angst are not prerequisites for being an artist. Sometimes artists operate on a very high frequency of creative energy and output. The all art, all the time energy needs a healthy balance. This can be the struggle of a comedic genius, who is driven to make the world a happier place, and to despair. The intensity of high-energy work and high-quality output is both a gift and a burden, resulting in excessive euphoria and melancholia. Great artistry can be the product of emotional excess and an extreme personal impulse to express and excel. It is known that the areas of the brain associated with emotion are highly active in exceptionally creative individuals. To avoid burnout, the energy needs to be balanced.

Another stereotype, the creative artist-individual can be seen as selfish with an ego that drives expression and behavior. Every artist is different, and there are probably a few on the planet who fit that description. More than ego, artists have enthusiastic creative confidence and skills to express themselves in new and different ways. In my survey, most of the artists I know are happy, hard-working, and share the frustration of not enough creative time or income. The cliche of the starving artist reflects the self-sacrifices of being employed in a field that fits their talents. Professional artists working in their medium get maker feedback, in applause and critique, that validates the work and prompts a continuum. A working artist doesn't discern their career from everyday living. Many music teachers teach full time, give private lessons, perform with groups at community events, and then relax at home with more music. A working artist must be entrepreneurial with self-discipline that supports a freelancer lifestyle. They know how to get the gigs and grants that support their craft and turn disadvantages into advantages. Artists are adept at making and adjusting their work to fit the context and resources available. The artist seeks to express the self FULL, which requires doing the hard work to make art and keep making art. Artwork is work.

Remarkably gifted artists are the visionaries and geniuses among us who change consciousness and illuminate the human condition. Pure genius is otherworldly, an enigma of rare and odd gifts that are inborn or acquired by life experience. Through nature or nurture, a genius has a ferocious dedication to hard work with a superhuman drive to keep up a productive routine that leads to mastery. Sometimes this hyper-focused willpower overrides all priorities, including wellness. A creative genius may be totally unique without healthy boundaries which often keeps them on the outside. Being an outsider is a freedom that allows for the mental space needed to do what has never been done before, to gestate and build a big idea uninhibited by interruption. This isolation can be voluntary or imposed, and often is a state of otherness that *motivates* creativity. Ultimately, the audience decides who or what is genius, which reflects a cultural consensus about the artist and artwork. Eccentric and enigmatic, some of the brightest geniuses were unrecognized during their lives until they posthumously gifted us with their brilliant works.

Visionary artists join scientists on the frontiers of thought and invention, transcending the motherlode of conventional design and knowledge to discover something original. They leave the status quo and collective culture to try to understand and envision the essence of all things. These rare individuals are the nonconformists and truth-sayers who challenge dogma within a societal or intellectual structure. They are passionate observers and changers of what is and what can be. Artists and scientists share a perceived eccentricity that allows for abstract thinking and discovery. Throughout history, they've been aligned with the despots who speak out for freedom and change and are often the first to be persecuted as revolutionaries. The writer's pen, filmmaker's lens, painter's brush, poet's phrase, and musician's song - artists use their tools on the front lines, telling their truth, and speaking with the universal language of art in ways that inspire hope and transformational change. It is ironic, artistic and gifted people can be envied and even hated by those who don't understand or relate to them. Don't hate the artists! Embrace, don't resent, their masterful talents. Artists criticize by creating because when the truth is exposed, it makes the world a better place, though some may not forgive them. Art raises its voice when power is corrupt. Art teaches and leads, and artists must be free within a society to express what is true and different. We must value and support the weirdly wise and wonderful artists among us who are born with a genius that enlightens the world.

We are all creative people. The conceptual divide between creatives and non-creatives can be bridged by equalizing the standard by which everyone's creativity is supported and esteemed. Humanistic self-actualization and self-expression are how we build human capital, because when we creatively empower individuals, we strengthen our society. A positive humanitarian shift towards prioritizing creativity in our personal lives and communities, and integrating it in education, health, commerce, and government, could just be the dawning of the Age of Aquarius when we each stand in our sovereign creative power, harmoniously together. This century will be transformed by creative technologies that unite the world and exalt individual capacities. Globally, the creative individualism of each person is good for the whole population, with you being you and me being me, with mutual respect for all regardless of age, gender, race, sexual orientation, religion, or socio-economic status. We are co-creators.

The emergent creative revolution is a faster way to better. A good creative ecology = a good creative economy. This is the planet's way to a future of abundance and universal wellness. The wellness of the individual reflects the wellness of the tribe. Whole people = whole Earth. All people need a creative life. Flourishing happens for everyone, everywhere, every day when creativity is recognized, nurtured, and valued by our collective society. The world needs all kinds of creators, and no human creature should ever believe that they are uncreative or unappreciated. It takes that needed shift in societal views and collective recognition of the value of creativity. The emerging wellness paradigm will uplift and positively transform all people as we realize our fullest creative potential and authentic power.

Creative people are hopeful and have a vision of the future. We are creators, not destroyers. From seed to soil to flower to fruit to harvest to seed again, the cycle of creativity is a generative and regenerative process. It is the energetic life force that *moves* us to think, do, and be. Let's relook at the *Creative Being.* It models this interaction and the power of the creative individual in action and aligned with all the cosmos. Again, visualize that the singular figure and the animated *motion* it implies is YOU, activating your native confidence to create. YOU, self-actualized and self-expressed, standing in your creative power with purpose and passion. Happy, healthy, and liberated in mind-body-spirit. YOU, radiating like a crystalline prism of light in the flow of creativity that springs from love and your center, a creative being, being creative. YOU with your creative true voice saying, "I am creative." This is creative equipoise. Your authentic power and native confidence to create is waiting for you to know it, claim it, nurture it, love it, and be it in the world. YOU are the one you've been waiting for. Believe it and achieve it. Become the artist-in-residence in your healthful, artful life.

18: Creative Practice

Like a fingerprint, the way we perceive and practice creativity is unique to each of us. Creative perception sparks the senses and starts the process. It is the impulse that enlivens. Creative practice mindfully *moves* the activity and does the work that defines a point of view. Being present in the experience is essential to benefitting from the practice. A conscious presence engenders personal growth and well-being. We have to participate in the action and reaction, to be in it, immersed in the flow of creative thinking, doing, and being. The process isn't stagnant or boring. It is a self-nurturing, self-*motivated*, self-aware activity that generates and regenerates the flow of expression. When we make creative practice part of our personal routine, wellness happens.

Doing creativity daily builds a positive growth mindset and proactive focus for living. Do what you know and love. A dose of Vitamin C-reativity is a good way to practice self-care. The systematic effort builds confidence, skills, and vitality. The key to maintaining a creative practice is taking the me-time needed to do it. A promise to self is to schedule personal time when you are unburdened by demands and unhurried. Slow and steady. Develop a system or method that works and keeps you learning and leaning into the process.

To get started, just *move*. Creativity is a work in progress that flows with the natural rhythms of life. The practice is a repetitive activity that requires doing it and having the patience to keep improving and working on your craft. Artwork is work. We can master a practice and the knowledge and skills needed to achieve our highest potential. This level of personal discipline requires an openness to expression and a commitment to do it.

"Practice" means not quitting and always giving your best effort. Desire must be greater than your resistance to avoid creative atrophy. Creativity is one of our strongest muscles. The more we use it, the stronger it gets. Muscles have memory, so if you haven't used your creative might for a while, brush off the dust and get back into the habit. Do it and be creatively fit for life.

Creative practice is often cathartic and challenging. It's important to trust the process and resist negative thinking and habits. Inner and outer critics may help or hinder. It is natural to self-evaluate and get instruction from others. Learn from the process and experience. Remember, we are perfect in our imperfections. Go with it. Take risks, make mistakes, and experiment. Trust, without restraint. Discover the parameters or lack of constraints that work with your creative style. It is not about being the best, it is about being your best self. Take pride in your original expression. The need for perfectionism may improve the craft, but when it is the only measure, it can kill creativity. If you feel some discomfort in the process this is a good thing, because it means you are still growing and developing skills. Mostly, let inner wisdom guide what works, and don't become attached to any judgment, good or bad. Have patience and courage. There is purity in unskilled efforts. Be the artist-in-residence, treat your work like art. It is not so much the thing, but the expression of the thing. Do creativity for you, not for status or approval. Pleasing others inhibits selfhood. The freedom of pure expression doesn't need any authority other than your appreciation and enjoyment. Practice creativity, not out of a sense of duty to others, but for personal wellness. It is not selfish to be creative, it is the self FULL.

Creative practice is both process and product. The novelty of something new and useful inspires the product, however, it's the process that makes it a work of art. It takes showing up and rolling up your sleeves to do the needed and desired work. A creative practice is "come as you are" and be yourself in the moment. It takes incubation, preparation, and putting it all together. A creative practice doesn't happen in isolation. As singularly as it manifests, the individual needs a communal relationship. Doing creativity is a singular or shared process, and it's always a collaboration, a synthesis of everyone and everything that makes it happen. We are co-creators who work in a synergistic relationship with our thoughts, feelings, ideas, habits, materials, books, methods, themes, environments, schedules, peers, instructors, and opportunities. We copy and model, innovate and originate, work solo and collaborate. Fellowship is a dynamic of human creativity. It's always okay to ask for help to create.

We get support from the resources, tools, and people who inspire our lives. We are supported by nature, an unconditional partner that activates the senses and connects us to the life force energy. Co-creators help us find our creative true voice. They are the teachers who instruct with no instruction and guide us toward self-discovery and self-expression. They don't do the work for us, they facilitate our efforts. There is much to be said about getting the encouragement needed to practice creativity. A teacher, whether it is your middle school art teacher or a parent, can instill self-confidence and self-discipline that lasts a lifetime. A good teacher embraces the student's level of skill and provides tools and methods to go beyond the lesson with self-directed learning and practice. In balance, we need co-creators and the interaction with external energy in a symmetric or asymmetric dynamic, whatever order or chaos that finds the need and follows intention. Co-creators are what and who supports creativity.

Naturally a part of creative practice, mindfulness is a life-enhancing skill. The brain loves creative meditation and is our brilliant co-creator in the process. Creative mindfulness is the ZONE, the fragrant and fertile garden of the open mind. It is a way to cultivate the flow and pure liberation of creativity. We can practice creative mindfulness by going to an art gallery, listening to music, working on a craft or hobby, making a pot of chili, taking a bubble bath, going for a walk, being in nature, or keeping a journal. We can go away by staying in place. It's a healthy daily habit that allows for time and space to clear the mind and open the heart. Clearing the mind refreshes the body and strengthens the spirit. Opening the heart is how to become the vessel for the creative source and consciously fill our cup of life, empty it, and fill it again with the joy of living in the moment. This heightened state of creative flow leads to mastery and promotes enjoyment in every aspect of the experience. We can envision creativity with focused visualizations that improve our work, relationships, and everyday living.

Creative mindfulness is an active process that helps maintain a healthy balance while doing what we love. Paying attention, on point, in full mind-body-spirit empowers creativity. The mindfulness of doing one thing with focused energy and intention can fuel a project or idea. It takes being present to do the work of creativity and continuing to show up. It takes time and concentration, slow and steady. Creative mindfulness is strengthening and enriching. It is a practice we look forward to doing.

Solitude can be an aspect of creative mindfulness. Taking me-time to be with yourself, and really BE, is a gift of being alone. Alone is being all one. It is an important relationship to the soul that lets thoughts and feelings flourish. In quietude, we can hear the call of our creative true voice. Tune out to tune in.

When mindfulness is directed toward a creative practice, we gain insights and the abundant gifts of our sentient nature. Giving full attention to the one-pointed mind is a way to enjoy simple activities and find peaceful pleasure in the process. This is the pathway to mastering any task or skill because, like the archer who hits their mark, the creative mind is brilliant when focused on one thing.

Creative mindfulness is activated by the senses. What we see, hear, touch, smell, taste, and intuit imprints itself in the moment and memory of the moment. The senses are our co-creators in every creative practice. These are sensory ways to practice creativity.

SIGHT - Active looking and seeing with the eyes and mind's eye. Perceive tones and shades of color. Observe lines, shapes, details, spaces, vistas of nature. Glimpse the light and all it illuminates. See near and far, inside and outside. Look to see to remember to enjoy. Visualize.

SOUND - Active listening. Be mindful of vibrations in and around you. Listen to nature's symphony. Make and listen to music. Resonate with life rhythms. Hear the sound of your pencil *moving* and heart beating. Tune-in to sound. Speak with creative true voice. Harmonize.

TOUCH - Feel with mind-body-spirit. Notice what touches you and is palpable. Try tactile exploration of pattern, texture, and form. Smooth or rough, cool or warm, wet or dry. Touch the Earth and absorb the sensation. Make physical contact with what you think and feel. Connect.

SMELL - Breathe deeply. Fill your lungs with the infusions of life. Inhale and exhale. Find fresh air and a fragrant environment. Smell the scents of the natural world with full olfactory stimulation. Saturate your senses with everyday perfumes and pleasing aromas for therapy. Oxygenate.

TASTE - Savor the flavor of what you eat and the creative things you love with gusto. Taste nature's abundance and sustenance. Satisfy your appetite and thirst for self-expression. Partake in the present and celebrate. Spice your food and life recipe to taste. Nourish.

INTUIT - Go with the sensory flow of the creative source. Observe your inner world. Be mindful, aware, sentient. Pay attention. See with your mind's eye. Go with what you know and feel. Trust and unconditionally open your heart to love and joy in the moment. Awaken.

A creative practice is often a peak creative experience. Doing creativity every day can be something you love and look forward to, an intimate and ultimate pleasure. Mine is keeping a sketchbook by my side so I can always capture an idea or drawing of the moments and scenes I observe. Artists often keep sketchbooks that are a collection of visual observations. It is the way to mindfully study an object or scene, and to draw what they see or imagine. It develops brain-eyes-hands skill and mastery. A painter usually has sketchbooks full of drawings for visual reference and exploring ideas.

Over the years, I've made creative wellness journals from the drawing and writing that flowed through me. They reflect what I was thinking, feeling, and seeing. I have one sketchbook that became a journal of my daily trips on the New York City subway when I lived and worked there, decades ago. Sketching was my creative meditation whenever I'd take the train. Mostly, I drew when lucky to get a seat, but sometimes standing. It was a travelogue that helped me see the beautiful diversity of New Yorkers commuting in the subway on their daily routines. Intrigued by this viewpoint, I imagined the stories of the people I sketched. I used a 6 x 9-inch sketchbook and a black pen. Because the train was *moving* and stopping, the portraits I sketched of the passengers were rhythmic, like the wheels running on the tracks. The sketchbook was my creative wellness journal and a peaceful place that felt like home. I looked forward to drawing in it, especially at the end of a busy work day when I was tired and stressed. Drawing is my way to wellness and happiness. The drawings I made on the New York subways taught me to observe the moment and how to draw on the go! Look to see to remember to enjoy the simple moments of life in *motion*.

The way to practice creativity is to do what you know and love. Think, do, be, imagine, muse, make, invent, innovate, explore, express, and experience. Do one creative thing every day. Creative practice is *motivated* by a positive intention to learn something new and take on a challenge. What are the steps to your creativity? How do you get started? Will you make doing it a daily practice? Creativity is a healthy habit for life that we need to *practice, practice, practice* - not because it's a way to get to Carnegie Hall - creative practice is a way to wellness.

19: Co-creators

Co-creators collaborate to make creativity happen. These are the people, places, things, ideas, and circumstances that get it in *motion*. There is fellowship in the process with everything and everyone that influences a creative practice and point of view. Most importantly, our resources and abilities are essential to when, where, and how we do creativity. It's always okay to ask for help to create.

Preparing the time, space, and tools to do a loved creative thing is part of a healthy practice. The rituals and ways we make ourselves ready for the process are common sense aspects of doing creativity. Planning and foresight help set the mood and mode for activity. When prepared, the process is more fluid and productive. Depending on the creative practice, taking inventory and engaging co-creators is how we think it through and control the process. Creativity is always a work in progress. Yes, artwork is work, which requires incubation, preparation, and putting it all together. Ask a great chef; they know a savory sauce takes prepping the right ingredients and cooking methods to create alchemy.

TIME, SPACE, and TOOLS are basic to every creative process. We can design our lifestyles to support the creative things we love to do. We enlist our executive mind to manage the technical aspects by prioritizing time, organizing space, and utilizing tools that facilitate our creative will. This is how to get creativity done. The following describes simple ways to get organized and start doing it. Because doing creativity is fun, I've included one of the most loved co-creators, PLAY. Be playful. Prepare to create. You can do it!

TIME

Time to start doing creativity. *Time...aye, there's the rub.* Perchance to have some for yourself to do your loved creative thing? Dream no more, time can be yours in the moment by claiming your creative power. Creative people know how to take me-time for a healthy dose of Vitamin C-reativity. The more time dedicated to creative wellness, the more well we'll be. We can balance life's chaos with a livable order by designing time for creative self-care through self-expression. Sounds ideal, but when will you ever have the time? That is a good first question.

Take pause, look at your life in balance. How much of your time is creative? Examine your lifestyle. Can you cultivate creative habits that enhance well-being and balance living? You'll need some me-time to contemplate these questions and *move* your energy towards self-care. *Me-time* in real-time. This is a big modern challenge. It takes time to get time, and we have too much to do and too little time. The responsibilities of work and social relationships occupy most of our active hours. It's not about having the time, it's about making time just for yourself and creative thinking, doing, and being in the moment, in your own time. It took time to become overwhelmed by stress and the daily grind, so it takes a span of hours to wind down and catch up.

We all need cycles of time that are a personal refuge and void of distractions. Scheduling restorative time when you can lose yourself to time, without a sense of guilt or duty to others, reduces stress and expands self-awareness. Time-out for time-in. Personal time opens the heart to creative flow. The art of being alone in intimate moments of fertile solitude can bring insights that nurture ideas and growth. Find an oasis of expressive time to refresh the creative well and make yourself FULL. This is not selfish.

Preparing and filling the creative well requires wellness time. A time to BE and let the true voice of "I need and desire" harmonize with the mantra "I am creative". Feeling free to take time may mean that you have to re-evaluate the balance of your work, play, and rest, and prioritize personal wellness. This can be difficult, to give to ourselves in a creative way when more often we are doing for others.

Young people naturally spend more time developing and expressing creative individualism. Often, by middle-age, many people tend to feel a lack of personal time and creativity in their lives. A huge population is aging that will need to find ways to occupy retirement and remain creatively relevant. We don't need to wait until we retire or have a chunk of free time to be creative. Sometimes people wait their entire lives to have personal time to do their creativity, then they get distracted or remain passive to their self-expression. Remember that you don't get time back, so when you have it, use it well. Procrastination inhibits productivity, especially when free time is limited. Maximizing time exalts the process.

It's proactive to have a plan and be prepared for creative practice. Generally, people tend to direct their time and activities toward personal preferences. Good time economy means managing daily living to include episodes of expression in equilibrium with personal habits, responsibilities, and relationships.

The more we collectively value creativity in all aspects of daily living, the more we will prioritize the time required for the experience. The times are changing and this is a good thing. Time + balance + you = wellness. Time is a co-creator when we do creativity.

SPACE

Our creative time needs to occupy a space. The vast regions of the creative mind give us plenty of room to roam amid the landscapes of the imagination. Mind space or physical space, our creative presence is the place where thoughts and feelings are expressed. We all need a place to put creativity, a spot where it can happen. Private or public environments where we can be actively creative are generally safe and nurturing. Schools, cultural organizations, workplaces, community venues, travel destinations, and natural settings offer creative spaces to occupy. Personal creative spaces include the home and intimate places where we are truly present with ourselves, others, and the environment. At home, a personal creative space can be any area dedicated to our interests.

Space economy is a consideration. It is great to have a studio or part of a spare room or garage, though it is not essential and a luxury for most creative projects. Sometimes having a free space means cleaning-up an area that is stagnant and cluttered. Making order gives more space for creative chaos. Crafters and do-it-yourselfers automatically claim their realms within the home. You can build a micro "you-topia" within an environment that provides an outlet for self-expression. This could be an easy chair with good lighting and books close at hand. *Move* things around and find some room, or go to the place where you can do your loved creative thing.

Start with what you have and design creative harbors in your life where you are the artist-in-residence. Whatever your space is, clean or cluttered, make it a place to organize and do creativity. Creative people can adapt their expression to fit a space or particular venue, and will make work to a scale that fits into that structure. A composer considers who will listen to the music and where it will be heard, then creates a composition that may rock a sports stadium filled with thousands of people, or gently rock a baby to sleep. Where, when, why, and for whom creativity happens can determine the context and process for expression.

One unconditional space to claim for expression is a blank page in a journal. Oh, the wonders of a blank page! A common writing or sketching journal can be a perfect place for your creative presence. A space to visit and revisit that goes wherever you go. Journal pages can contain our thoughts, emotions, ideas, inspirations, images, stories, poetry, memories, dreams, lists, and notes to self. The one-dimensional space of a page can be transformed into a two-dimensional reference for personal expressions and histories. It can be three-dimensional with pop-up, folded, or collaged pages. On the creative journey, a journal is a way to have a reliable companion and space within the wide-open acreage of flat paper surfaces. Considering the cost of real estate, it is an efficient, self-contained place to create. It is like a studio in a book. Beyond a book, a journal can also be a series of photographs, videos, musical compositions, or multimedia visual art. The healthy habit of keeping a journal holds the time and space for creativity. A journal establishes a point of view, and we can return to that view each time we look back at this one-of-a-kind volume. It is a receptive space for personal expression that is safe and freeing and a creative task we look forward to doing. Journaling is a vehicle for selfhood that highlights our interests and what is relevant in life at any moment.

A blank page, kitchen table, cozy corner, dance floor, or room with a view. Wherever it is, space is a co-creator where we do creativity.

TOOLS

Creative tools are how we do the tasks we love. These are the implements that help advance interests and hone skills. The range of apparatus is as diverse as we are creative. A sketch, recipe, mind map, plan, or how-to reference can get the job done. Tools are devices, guides, or processes for doing creativity. They are instrumental in how we manifest and facilitate our inspired will.

If there is something creative you would like to do, but don't have the tools needed, then try an expression that is less technical. Keep it simple. Do what you can. A creative practice is a natural skill. It should be within your resources and abilities and not require special training or be too difficult or expensive to produce. Creative people know how to be frugal innovators. We know what's on-hand and how to make do to do what we love. The process is organic and improvised as necessary. It's about doing it yourself and using common things to create something uncommon.

Tools help us do the work of creativity. The better the tools the more we can improve our craft. We can take classes and do research to support self-directed learning. While cultivating interests, we discover the tools needed and can enjoy acquiring them. Buying materials helps us better understand the medium or tasks at hand. The internet is a resource to explore and shop for tools and products. Artists who buy art supplies in bricks and mortar art stores are often buying them from artists who are employed there. Over many years of investigating materials, the artists I've met at local art supply stores have been a resource for learning how mediums work and the technical tools required. I also learn about materials from my artist friends and basically we all say, "Try it, see what works for you." If your creativity is fly fishing, then likely you know the network that offers the gear to outfit the adventure and outwit the fish.

When preparing, one of the best tools to get creativity started and advance projects is a "to do list". Writing a list and outlining a strategy with a timeline gets energy and intention focused toward goals and desired outcomes. Don't be shy about listing all the tools and steps that can efficiently map out a creative process. This will greatly impact how well you use the time and space available for a project. One thing about a list is to remember to have it on-hand when shopping for tools. In the spirit of things written by hand and remembered, I've scribed many lists that I've forgotten or lost. Still, because I made the mental inventory it all came together, and when creative time arrived, I was ready and equipped.

A way to prepare for creative practice is to make a customized creativity kit with the tools needed for personal expression. Creative tools may include colored pencils or a camera, any hands-on thing that makes your creativity happen. It could be as simple as a museum membership card in your wallet and a pair of walking shoes. When organizing your creativity kit, include any infusions that muse the creative spirit. My kit reflects that I'm a painter. In plein air style, I have an L.L. Bean tote bag with a set of watercolors, brushes, small cup, cotton cloth, watercolor paper, drawing materials, sketch pad, bottle of water, and a snack. Creativity to go. I can take it to an outdoor location, a friend's weekend camp, or any room in my house. All the expressive tools I need in a contained and portable space, awaiting my precious focused time. This is my arts medicine bag, my ready remedy and way to creative wellness.

Gather and acquire what you need for self-expression. Tools are co-creators that implement how we do creativity.

PLAY

Let's PLAY! Basically, doing what we love feels like play because it *moves* energy in ways that calm or rouse with beneficial effect. The practice of play frees the flow of creativity. Mind-on, body-on, spirit-on fun is a peak creative experience. It gives an uplifting sense of satisfaction, accomplishment, and enjoyment. Spending time with children, taking dancing lessons, hobbies or crafting, home improvement projects, traveling to another time zone, learning a new skill, deep listening to music, being a dedicated sports fan, or delighting in a romantic date. These are ways to practice original play and simple spontaneous acts of self-expression.

We can play alone because our imagination is always game. Often we are co-creators in the act of play with our friends, cohorts, teammates, or community groups who share our passions and interests. These are our playmates.

Free and innocent, creativity opens the childlike mind to wonder. A playful creative person is curious and seeks the awe and exhilaration of new experience. Albert Einstein said, "Play is the highest form of research." When we go out of our comfort zone to do something novel, we learn about ourselves and are rewarded with the gifts of whimsey. Creative people are never bored because they know how to amuse themselves and probably have a few toys to get the fun *moving*.

Play is instinctual in children and that free-spiritedness doesn't dim with age. From the cradle to grave, frolic and fun benefits our emotional, cognitive, social, and physical well-being. Sporting and cavorting makes us better abstract thinkers and problem-solvers, helps fine-tune motor skills, and teaches us to share and collaborate with others. It reduces stress and builds vitality. As we age, our playfulness is an attitude that can keep us curious and interested and makes life more fun. If you haven't played recently, dust yourself off, and jump back in the sandbox.

Play is our creative mojo, the energetic stuff that keeps us engaged, animated, and *moving*. Playfulness allows us to be naturally free-spirited and expressive. The process of play is part of nature's brilliant biological plan for creation because it organically enlivens the dopamine arousal of anticipation, pleasure, and reward. It's exciting, enjoyable, and enriching. The positive state of playfulness can be applied to virtually every aspect of life. It breaks the routine and compels us to action.

The act of play is spontaneous, though it can be a challenge to schedule the me-time needed to freely engage. Organize time, space, and tools to accommodate your favorite way to play. Pack a creativity kit and be ready for the adventure. Entertaining one's self and others with smiling moments of creative play builds confidence and social relationships.

Like a team sport, play values the individual's contribution to the whole. It *motivates* a competitive spirit that loves the dopamine rush of victory. The culture of play promotes a level of excellence by which skills are measured. The more we practice and improve our ability to play, the more we become expert players. When we practice original play we use our artifice to ingeniously burst out of the boring box of conformity to reinvent ourselves. Common things become uncommon with the alchemy of our free spirit in free play. Play engenders a sensory flow that animates the body with expression. It is creativity in action, part practice and lots of improvisation. The rules are basic. Show up, be nice, play fair, and be yourself at your best.

Playing requires creative presence and active participation in taking the moment and making it a moment. There are different ways to play because we all have a unique stake in the game. What I'm describing is free play your way. It is what makes you feel good, carefree, and happy. It enriches and refreshes. In its highest form, it is an organic process, without technology or artificial distraction, that connects the mind-body-spirit in a peak creative experience.

No more all work and no play. Live, work, play, and create in balance. Have fun. More play = more health and happiness. Play is an energizer of creative true voice. With the ecology of practice, it empowers the expressive experiences that make life less heavy and more happy. It gives us opportunities to be ourselves, plugged-in and unplugged. As the whimsical Irish writer Oscar Wilde (1854-1900) wisely mused, "Be yourself, everybody else is already taken."

Play is the thing and the stage for "I am creative". The act of play can free the parts of our expression that are stifled and blocked by all those things that play out in life. Play teaches, prompts, nurtures, expands, strengthens, entertains, connects, affirms, and releases. The operative word is FUN! Amuse and please yourself. Try tapping your inner playgirl or playboy. Maybe it's the best crazy thing that you will ever do or dream of doing. Do it for YOU. Follow this aliveness and the animated impulse to frolic. Push your PLAY button, and go with the flow of what happens. Maybe turn up the volume. Embrace the muse and step lively. Be in the imaginative playful moment. Do creativity for the fun of doing it.

Creative play requires a change in attitude and *moving* your energy in an experience that engages and excites. Take a day off, open your journal, go for an adventure with a friend, try that new recipe, step onto the dance floor. Game on! You've got this one. Enjoy your toys and playmates. Play is a co-creator, easy and fun.

YOU CAN DO IT!

Take a pledge and make a promise to self to practice your everyday creativity as a way to wellness. Write a few sentences that will *motivate* you to be the artist-in-residence in your healthful, artful life. Reflect on what you are learning through *ART HOPE* and all the ways to create wellness. Describe your creativity and set goals for becoming your best creative self. Sign and date your pledge and keep it as a reference and reminder to do the creative things you love to do.

Consider making a creative to do list. This is easy and helps get the process started. Keep the list updated as you achieve creative goals and finish projects. It can be therapeutic and enjoyable to check things off the list once creative tasks are completed and to add new ones. Most importantly, have fun. You can do it!

Part Four: Healing

20: Creative Resilience

The flow of creativity is naturally healing. You are a creative creature with the innate ability to self-express and self-heal. You have the ready remedy in your medicine bag. It is an inborn quality that can be tapped at any time, a reserve of vitality that responds to healing intention. Creativity doesn't miraculously fix every ill or problem, yet, it can be a heal-all salve that nurtures wellness and a good life. Creative energy naturally finds its way to what needs healing. It may sting when applied to wounds, or not. The process strengthens and restores with intuitive cures that promote homeostasis. The healing aspects of creativity are evident in how we feel. There is a release of energy that calms or rouses. This *movement* is essential to good health. Things that expand a personal sense of time and experience can be soothing, exciting, or a little of both. We tend to feel good when doing our loved creative thing. This positive energy affects health.

When a transformation occurs the health-enhancing effects of positive energy and belief are activated. It is the hope factor, a mighty elixir that works with intention and the power of mind-body-spirit. It *moves* energy at a cellular level, directing it toward what we want, need, and believe. The hope factor is interconnected to vital energy and chi that flows through meridians in the body. Chi is a term used in ancient Chinese medicine that describes the active force of life-giving energy. It is a founding concept for acupuncture and other energy healing traditions. In Hindu and Ayurvedic medicine it is known as prana, the life force energy that *moves* and animates every living thing. This positive energy activates sensory awareness and aligns with intention to create a healing balance.

Within each of us, the creative source is always alive and flowing. Sometimes, this vital energy can be dormant or blocked in a way that causes a deep wound. The natural flow of expression is not activated because it's disadvantaged in some way by physical, psychological, or environmental conditions. It's still bubbling up inside, waiting to be tapped, but things happen in life that cause creativity to be inert, unable to *move* with the natural rhythms of expression. When an aspect of life lacks creativity, in how we relate to ourselves, others, and the environment, it becomes stagnant and the vitality of nurture is neglected. What is the disconnect that causes this negative effect? The suppression of expression blocks the natural flow of life force energy. This can lead to depression, unhappiness, and severe illness. Some people lack creative expression in their lives because they've been conditioned to believe that they are not good at "art". In my expressive arts practice I've heard many workshop participants say, "I am not creative." Words no creature should ever speak! From suppressed to expressed, I offer this personal mantra, "I am creative." These three words can be the way to creative resilience and wellness.

A lack of expression or too much negative conditioning, whether internal or external, can have a placebo effect that causes creative atrophy. When there's a false perception our creativity isn't worthy or good enough, it doesn't develop and remains suppressed. Like life force energy, creativity responds to its environment, to the vitality of nurture or stagnation of neglect. Creative wounding is an intense form of trauma. It occurs during youth or adulthood. Negative life events and relationships, and unhealthy emotional and physical factors may dim but never extinguish our creative light. Creativity in the medicine bag is like having an emergency flashlight that shines on the wounded parts of ourselves that need self-examination and self-care. A resistance to creativity may reflect an aspect of life that needs healing. We all have light and dark sides. There is no shadow without light. Acknowledge the dark feelings and problems, with love and light, by befriending trauma and finding peace with all that was, is, and will be. This *moves* the blocked energy to transform and transcend fear, hurt, neglect, shame, guilt, and grief. It forgives and liberates the negative stigma encapsulated in the wound. Secrets can sicken. The pain of the past needn't paralyze the present. Trauma hides what is real. These hidden wounds can make us act contrary to what we know and need in ways that sabotage health and happiness. The deadly cycle of re-wounding continues. Releasing what doesn't best serve your highest potential, with forgiveness toward self and others, is how to reclaim personal power and the native confidence to create.

You are perfect in your imperfection. Everything that you are is enough, and you are not what happened to you. Recognize what happened and how surviving it makes you resilient. Survivors are defined by the integrity of being who they are, not by the dis-ease and stigma of traumatic life events. All your fragmented parts embody the whole beautiful person you are. Resilience is the will to shine again. Love is the glue that connects all those uniquely broken fragments and gives a glowing patina to your lived experience. Accept who you are, unconditionally. Faults, warts and all, you are complete. Let the flow of creativity *moving* wash away emotional toxins and nurture the connectedness and strength needed to *move* beyond the negative forces that obstruct expression and handicap wellness.

Creative resilience is like inner hands full of light pushing back the darkness. It gives hindsight to reflect on how far you've come and appreciate that it took courage to resolve to evolve. Like frozen winter snow that melts into the flowing waters of spring, the release and letting go is hopeful and enlivening. Resilience forgives and finds a way forward at a slow and steady pace with optimism and vitality. It is the liberation of accepting what can't be controlled and how hard truths have freed your creative true voice. Resilience is a way to remember the best of life, and pick up the threads to reweave and refine a tapestry of self. It takes unconditional trust and *moving* beyond what suppresses expression. Trust opens creative flow. It is like putting your pencil to the paper, and not stopping, until the mind releases and the heart unfurls.

It is not easy to undo the dysfunction and damage from physical and emotional traumas that steal expression and silence creative true voice. Enter the archetype of the shaman, the original artist-healer with supernatural abilities to observe and rhythmically balance life forces. Homeostasis requires a natural balance. In order to restore this harmony, a change in energy takes place, a healing transaction that *moves* and transforms the mind-body-spirit. A master physician and psychologist, the shaman helps make the Universe right. They bear witness to the pure essence of who we are. They see and *move* the energy in a symbolic ceremony of soul retrieval and liberation. The shaman is a metaphor for the chaos needed in order to change and claim creative power. The process involves loving and slaying psychic dragons, and courageously acknowledging and releasing the negative energy that suppresses wellness. Though difficult, we must believe in our wholeness and goodness.

Trauma can cause disembodiment, a type of self-abandonment when our mind disconnects from the body and estranges the spirit. After the fight, we need to rest. After the flight, we need to return, to become grounded and reclaim our wholeness. The strain of facing the pain is epic, as darkness dies to be reborn to light. Discourse, then the healing begins when we confront issues, accept the situation, and stay in relationship with our distress until we make the changes needed to grow and let go. This allows the harmonious flow of healing energy to *move* and soothe. We all need nurture and self-care, and must learn to practice empathy of self and direct love and compassion inward.

Though difficult, and often heartbreaking, it is important to eliminate negative environments, influences, and people to be well and happy, whatever the circumstances. It is necessary to make healthy boundaries and seek the support of close friends and family who are willing to be present and listen, and believe our story. Social and emotional connectedness with like-minded people builds trust and the confidence that it's okay to be ourselves. Empathy taps resilience. Having one kind human who will bear witness and offer comforting words and hugs, is how we can manage the emotional heavy-lifting. It's okay to ask for help to heal.

In order to maintain a dynamic aliveness, we must create new ways of thinking, doing, and being. Our presence in the process, as scary and daring as it may be, is fundamental to self-actualization and self-expression. Hardship happens, but don't be hard on yourself. Practice optimism and find ways to get out of your discomfort zone. *Move* beyond what hurts and holds you back. Be brave, the only way out is through. Navigating the ups and downs helps us know our strengths and vulnerabilities. Obstacles can be benefactors that inspire life and art and stimulate our natural healing gifts. An infirmity can affirm resiliency. Our wounds make us healers. The shaman archetype resembles the wounded healer. A trauma is transformed and healed, from breakdown to breakthrough. It follows the alchemy of how creativity transforms something common and ordinary into something uncommon and extraordinary. A transmutation of energy occurs that can take us to near death and back to life again. The sick psychic substance dies, to be reborn to health and balance. Something old is destroyed and something new is created. Life is reviewed and renewed.

The shaman is a wizard of the medial who dances between the physical and metaphysical, the conscious and unconscious. He acts like the pebble, the co-creator causing the change that affects the flow of life force energy. Transformative change happens in an instant and over time. Knowing that life is imperfect and changeable is freeing. Creativity is a way to resiliency, a form of shamanism that shakes things up with a primordial *motion* that opens self-awareness and activates creative power. It transforms a victim consciousness into a creator consciousness, from FEAR to LOVE. It requires accepting and allowing for the forgiveness and vulnerability that prompts taking a leap into life, with a fearless belief in one's self-worth and self-efficacy.

Creativity is a connective medium for making whole the fragmented parts of our psyche. The stress of coping with life trauma can force people to the edge, emotionally, physically, and socially. The otherness of marginalization provides a new perspective and impetus to express creativity. Psychological research suggests that people who suffered trauma can experience post-traumatic growth. This transforms adversity to advantage, prompting healthy optimism and creative confidence. A positive growth mindset and focused desire for an improved life are strong indicators of wellness in all aspects of living, and we all have this capacity.

The creative healer makes peace and finds sweetness in the woe, and knows that what doesn't kill us can make us stronger and wiser. Emotional pain can be put to good use. The pathway to resilience can be frustrating and exhausting. We need to have patience and slow down and only do what we can. The utility of resilience restores confidence and health, just by doing what works and feels good. During recovery from illness, trauma, or difficult times, creative resiliency skills can be learned to foster healthy responses and a positive perspective. Skills are developed through self-directed learning and finding resources and people to support the process. Co-creators who help us develop creative resiliency skills include healthcare providers, counselors, mentors, instructors, peers, and close friends and family.

The transformational energy of creativity has helped me throughout my life. I learned at a young age that it was better to be creative than to be unhappy and self-identified as an artist in my earliest expressions. It has always felt natural to express myself during life's important moments, mostly in pictures and words. For better or worse, my visual art making and writing have companioned me in the best and worst times of my average life. My creative body of work embodies who I am and is the vehicle for self-awareness that bears witness to my soul story. It reflects my observations, introspections, dreams, myths, visions, passions, hopes, and beliefs. I am grateful for this process, which requires me to muse with the shaman on many sunny nights and dark days. As it relates to my personal healing practice, I draw, paint, and write to sanctify my thoughts and feelings in a creative form. This is a ready and reliable remedy in my medicine bag. With art as my witness, I accept my flawed and fabulous self. A healthy self, heals thy self.

Creative resilience is an aspect of good health. I will never forget the description of how important creativity is to wellness told to me by a woman who was struggling with a long-term illness. She attended my drawing workshop at a hospital wellness center. In a guided visualization, I made the connection of feeling and embodying the charcoal medium on the paper. After a few meditative drawing exercises, the woman told me she felt the process opened the door to a room where she had left her creativity when disease changed her life. She put it there because it was too precious and she was too sick, so she isolated herself from that life-giving part of her being. The process of *moving* the charcoal helped her visualize going back into that room, where she had carefully stored her creativity, and bringing it back into herself. The psychophysical aspects of creating health help us visualize the healing we need.

Creativity activates the inner shaman and a trans-healing process takes place. Like meditation, prayer, joy, and love, the healing effects of creativity alter us at a cellular level. Healthy cells create healthy cells. The natural healer welcomes this life force energy to *move* through the mind-body-spirit vessel. We build immunity and health with this proactive growth, coupled with a positive attitude and good well care habits. Prioritizing health and well-being makes more health and well-being. Like nurtures like in rhythmic reciprocity. Positive creative intention can *move* our energy to create health.

As medical science gets closer to a cure for cancer they are discovering that immunotherapy is a way to treat the immune system by stimulating it to create more immune responses, more healthy life-giving cells that can fight and kill the disease. Our body has the ability to self-heal and generate what we require to create health. Immunotherapy uses our cellular function to change the killing mission of the oncogene that fuels cancer by brilliantly creating healthy cells that fight the predatory spread of the disease. This new horizon in cancer research is in contrast to the function of traditional chemotherapy, which uses chemical substances that are cytotoxic to kill the rapidly dividing cancer cells, and adversely, can also kill the healthy cells that the immune system generates. There is much to learn about how the resilient immune system creates health. Beginning with creating a healthy environment, personally and globally, is how we can heal at a cellular level. Nurturing health, creates health.

Creative resilience is an empowerment that comes with an acceptance of the ever-changing cycles of life, all the chaos that makes our personal order. Living in balance is parallel to homeostasis. It's important to go with the flow, and to consciously practice creative self-expression and self-care. The stresses of daily living need a release. We all have a timeline and personal process for wellness that needs our attention and nurture, not neglect. The natural healer dwells at the threshold of our creative thinking, doing, and being, when we are present in mind-body-spirit. From dystopia to utopia, ultimately the goal is balance. Your wellness is your own creation. The overarching emotion that determines wellness is a sense of happiness, which is one of the most important indicators of health and well-being. Happiness happens when we are hopeful and resilient. It is the best remedy for any ailment. Smiling is a symptom of creative wellness. Smile and wink at the shaman and tap the healing power of creativity.

21: ART HOPE

Creativity + life = art. Faith + love = hope. These balancing factors inspire wellness and happiness, and are why I've written *ART HOPE*. As I reflect on my own process, from the seed of an idea to the words on these pages, with all of my heart I believe that art + hope = healing. It is a labor of love and pure stick-to-itiveness, a work of passion fused with purpose that has blessed my being. Through the ups and downs of writing and rewriting, of taking it all in and letting it all out, I've discovered my own creative resilience and come to understand the soul-strengthening hard work of belief. I've learned that art and hope are co-creators, the pebbles that start the flow and *move* still waters. Whether sad or happy, difficult or easy, what happens in life happens in the studio, we create what we live.

Art is every product of human creativity. It is a universal force for good that animates and **art**iculates our individual and collective expressions. Being the artist-in-residence in your life promotes a positive growth mindset and productivity. Creativity has a balancing effect that supports wellness. It makes you take time to do what you love and make a life, not just make a living. It is about being, not having, and about being happy and having hope because creativity provides healing opportunities and abundance. Art is a medium for creative equipoise that defines individualism, increases vitality, promotes learning, gives pleasure, and celebrates living. Everything ever created and all we create is in our DNA. Art doesn't imitate life, it enlivens and illuminates it. Art is life.

Creative true voice is your personal art and life narrative. If I've expressed mine well, *ART HOPE* will help you recognize and express yours. When it speaks, listen. It is the sound of the creative source flowing, heard with all the senses and felt with the heart. It announces, "I am creative." This is how to make life a masterpiece, a work of art like no other. Your creative true voice is not afraid to do what you love and live the life you are meant to love. It tells your true story. The Universe values this verse. Individual truth is always subjective and has a pure resonance that affirms life with a feeling of faith only the believer can describe. Art is the refuge of creative true voice and universal truth, a keeper of integrity and what is believed. Like an inner compass that points to true north, creative true voice must truly reflect your thoughts, feelings, and beliefs. Sometimes truth is like a missile that bombs the status quo and is not what others want to hear or see. In each truth, the opposite is equally true. Speak and be your truth, and never let anyone disparage who you are and what you believe. We can be tolerant and remain peaceful when we don't allow our creativity to be suppressed or silenced. Speaking with creative true voice is an expressive way of opening to new wisdom and experience.

BE and become your art. Stay true to your voice and express it with creative confidence and clarity. From order to chaos, change is the only constant in the Universe, and one can only change one's self. Change comes from within, as we invent and reinvent ourselves through the cycles of time and expanses of space in our lives. We are resilient creative creatures, not destroyers. Creativity is a positive force, not a frailty. It comes from love, not fear or hate. It uplifts the human condition and often rises up from the ashes like a phoenix fueled by life's biggest challenges, greatest loves, and deepest knowing. When we have the courage to speak with creative true voice, we can understand and express the meaning of life with purpose and passion. Inspired in mind-body-spirit, we aspire to make something beautiful and practical. We are gardeners who nurture and enjoy the fruits of labor. We are creators who create a better world.

Love is creative. Loving and being loved opens the flow of creativity. Like a free fall into love, creativity requires taking risks and letting go. Trust this enlivened flow, lean into it to see what the Universe offers. The artistic free will to express with an open heart can *move* us to create something of value for ourselves and others. Inspired by love, we express thoughts and feelings, needs and desires. Because we love, we create our best lives. Creativity is how we feel and express love. An artist mentor of mine wore a necklace with beads that spelled, *art loves you*. She would jiggle them and smile as she offered her cure-all blessing and a hug. The love of self-nurture and self-care through creative self-expression is healing. It is always there to affirm and comfort, a ready remedy in the medicine bag. Yes, art loves you.

We celebrate love with an enthusiastic attitude of gratitude in life's most important moments. The art of celebration is a way to honor the people and things we love most. Being grateful is the grail full. It is an expression of positive feelings and how we show appreciation. Children are naturally open in how they express creative gratitude. It is evident in their whimsical art that reflects pure emotion and wisdom beyond youth. Like empathy, it is not just something we feel, it is what we do. Gratitude is an act of affirmation and belief that expresses the story of love. It is important and pleasurable to express it, and often. Similar to the benefits of love and creativity, gratitude reduces stress, nurtures social relationships, promotes optimism, and engenders a state of grace. Gratitude shines a light on the blessings of abundance and gifts that enrich living every day. It is a healthy practice to appreciate who and what we care about. Sometimes, we feel a lack of abundance and wellness because of emotional imbalance or negative circumstances that steal our plentitude. Creativity nourishes what we lack and restores a healthy balance.

Art is a way to communicate what matters and what we believe. It gives us a universal language to speak out against oppression, violence, hatred, and injustice with a creative true voice. Art is a way we respond to love, hope, beauty, and life that speaks to who, what, and why we are. It is impossible to imagine a world without art. If we awakened one day and it happened, I believe, within minutes of the sun rising, artists will rise up to create anew. As citizen artists, we will tap our creative resilience and talents, and the arts will be seeded to flourish and enrich life again. Art is the highest form of hope.

When the COVID pandemic shocked the world population into quarantine, isolation, deep grieving, and uncertainty, we rose together to bear witness and share our love and stories through the arts. Creativity is the ready remedy and the way forward as we innovate and improve our lives. There are many unknowns still looming about what our post-pandemic world will be. It is a Me to We moment, when we are called to come together with compassion, tolerance, and the ability to adapt and evolve our human condition. I feel hopeful and believe that our collective human creativity will prevail and usher in a new age of science and public health, entrepreneurism, wellness education, social consciousness, and human kindness. We must believe in our recovery and know that we are doing it collectively.

The "hope factor" is created by healthy optimism and positive belief. This life-affirming energy makes more good energy and *moves* the believer towards what is believed. Hope is not about getting what we want, it is about getting what we believe, and it's not about wanting things because the best things in life are not things. The positive intention of belief stimulates the hope factor's affirmative placebo with powerful effect. If we believe we are well, we will be well. If we believe in our creativity, we will be creative. The law of attraction says good energy makes good energy, and bad energy makes bad energy. Cause and effect. This is a basic philosophy of wellness - to maintain positive balance, intention, and belief.

Our actions are inspired by what we believe and the people who believe in us. To engender the stamina of hope, it only takes one person who "sees" you and believes in your creativity. Someone who offers kind words of encouragement when it is needed most. People who believe in you are the tribe where you belong and feel safe. They are the friends, teachers, mentors, and close relations who recognize your strength of character and cheer you on. They show up to care and be present in your life. These people are not the haters, wet-blanket throwers, or jealous nay-sayers. They love and appreciate your unique talents and quirky ways. Hope is a desire for well-being and happiness that is often hard-won. Trust yourself and remain resilient. Ultimately, your happiness is not based on other people. It is inside your heart and in the simple things that bring joy to life. Happiness happens when we accept ourselves and the way things are, one beautiful day at a time.

A good attitude is the touchstone of hope. Fearless creative confidence and vitality transcends toxic doubt and negative influences. Hope feels like our purpose and passion. It is our strongest belief and most desired wish. Hope is a deep yearning for good and seeing the good in all things. It is a thing we have and do. We hopefully dream and enter the realm where our gifts and potential are exalted. Sometimes our creative dreams inspire us to do the impossible. When we keep the faith those dreams are possible. Expectant, we hold onto our dreams, and we may fall, but when we fly, we soar beyond expectations. Hope rises like a light on the horizon. It comes in a window of opportunity to give warmth and the resolve to embrace resilience, even as we embrace uncertainty and certain challenges.

Hope is a call for change that brings evolution or revolution. It takes grit, the organic substance in the soul that keeps us rooted in our belief. Hope can be exhausting, frustrating, and worrisome. Yet, it eclipses fear and keeps us looking forward with positive anticipation and *motion* towards good outcomes. Like creativity, hope is intuitive and open-minded, nurtures self-esteem, and gives voice to ideas and emotions. It is a type of intelligence that keeps us in a perpetual present looking toward the future. It requires patience, steadfastness, and time. Through the empathic lens of creativity, hope reminds us that grace exists at every level of human experience. Hope faithfully teaches the principles of healthy optimism and to aim high with an unconditional belief in a good outcome.

A crisis can be a healing opportunity. A happy and hopeful creative person turns life's obstacles into benefactors. With a positive attitude and the courage to work hard, we make good choices, maintain confidence in our abilities, and resolve to keep trying, again and again. Success in life is directly related to unconditional trust in our capacities. Creative believers are idealistic and not limited by nonbelievers. We dream it and do it with passion. Creative believers are successful because we persist and never give up until a goal is reached. We are able to overcome fear and come from love, to trust in ourselves and a higher power. Hope never slumbers, but desire must be greater than resistance. There is no plan B, only a better plan A.

Great things happen when we own our integrity and are affirmed by the faith others have in us. We glimpse divinity in the exceptionally gifted individual who rises above extreme difficulties to live their highest purpose in ways that uplift and inspire others. These remarkable people are the hope-givers who lead humanity to a higher consciousness through transformative acts of creative faith. They are the artists, scientists, thinkers, writers, teachers, mentors, parents, friends, athletes, leaders, revolutionaries, spiritualists, healers, and innocents whose exemplary actions make our world better.

Like waves in the ocean, the ebb and flow of hope and despair is evidence of a life well-lived. The highs and lows make us stronger, though sometimes the gravity of hopelessness weighs heavy. Because we are human, our hearts break and we feel bone-deep sadness. Life is that way. What can we do? How can we maintain hope and hold on to what we love and believe? Hold on, but loosely, because change is inevitable. It may be difficult to see that what is changing is for the better. Then, a tiny bit of light shines, and we realize it was always there. When we feel that we just can't go on, someone or something touches us. We have only to reach out. To ride the roughest tides it takes oceanic compassion and unconditional love of self. When eclipsed by the hardest, darkest times, there is a light we do not see. Be brave and open to positive potential. Hope is a healing opportunity if we trust the goodness of our intentions and belief.

Don't give up on yourself. The dialogue of hope can seem like hyperbole and tiresome speculation. It may not be what you want to hear or believe. It is not uncomplicated, and can get in the way of being present with the rawness of real emotion. Hopeful cliches and the idea that things will turn out right, someday, no matter what happens, often seem like platitudes when suffering. In troubled times hope can feel lost, like a forgotten part of the soul. Slow and steady, emerge when you are ready. The Universe remembers and believes you. It offers the gifts of resilience and assurance that you are in the place just right, even though it hasn't been a valley of love and delight. Living a full life, on your own terms, and not giving power to negative thinking and feeling, is a way to validate spiritual ownership and empower the future.

BE a creative change maker. DO what you believe in ways that better yourself and others. The Universe will affirm your faith and give a sign that resonates in mind-body-spirit when you are on a sacred pathway. I have experienced great joy when teaching watercolor classes at the cancer center. I've also shared the woes and suffering that some of my participants are going through. There is a synergy of positive energy and transference of hope within the group process that is profoundly healing. One day while teaching a watercolor class, I was feeling stressed and wondered if the hard work of my low-paying vocation was the right choice. A woman, who was a new participant in my class, announced to our group that she had recently lost her daughter to leukemia and was dealing with her own cancer diagnosis and chemotherapy. The process of painting relaxed her anxiety. She was visibly emotional. At the end of the program, as I looked at her artwork, the woman grabbed my hand, and quietly explained that the watercolor class was the best two hours she'd had in the past year. Recognize your angels. They remind us to believe, BE, and *move* forward. I was humbled, and my resolve strengthened to embrace my role as the animated art teacher and be the pebble, the inspired spark that *moves* people to express their creativity. When in doubt, ask for a sign. Be open to awe and the wonderment of divine timing. Affirmations of faith enlighten the darkest moments. To be happy and keep life in balance, we must remain hopeful and believe something wonderful is about to happen.

Artistic symbols of hope infuse cultural and religious traditions and personal spiritual iconography. Language, sound, and visual art mediums create symbolic imagery that expresses human resilience and hope for a brighter, happier tomorrow, with no more struggle and fear, only love and peace. Metaphors in words, music, and pictures that make hope iconic are a bird, a bridge, a boat, a horizon, a light, an angel, wings to fly. A season, a seed, a storm, a rainbow, a blossom, a fruit with a new seed. A need, a desire, a wish, a dream, a vision, a love, a blessing, a truth expressed. Art gives hope a form. We create what we believe. Symbols of hope give us the strength to overcome, no matter how bad it gets, with shining optimism and a commitment to faith that affirms life and the meaning of existence. Not everything works out as hoped, and so we jump into the fresh wellspring of creativity and remain resilient.

Practice your everyday creativity as the way to wellness. Begin with what you know, what you have, and what you love, from where you are, right here, right now. Art inspires art. Hope inspires hope. Believe it, and BE the artist-in-residence in your healthful, artful life. Strive and thrive on.

Part Five: Learn More

22: Inspiring Books

Here is a short inventory of the many books that inspired this work. They are all good for seeking, learning, and enjoying. Find books and let books find you.

Andreasen, Nancy. *The Creating Brain: The Neuroscience Of Genius.* New York: Dana Press, 2008

Babbitt, Edwin D. *The Principles Of Light & Color.* Secaucus, N.J.: The Citadel Press,1967.

Borysenko, Joan. *Guilt Is The Teacher, Love Is The Lesson.* New York: Warner Books, 1988.

_____. *Mind The Body, Mending The Mind.* Massachusetts: Addison Wesley, 1987.

Cameron, Julia. *The Artist's Way: A Spiritual Path To Higher Creativity.* New York: Tarcher Putman, 1992.

Campbell, Don. *The Mozart Effect: Tapping The Power To Heal The Body, Strengthen The Mind And Unlock The Creative Spirit.* New York: Quill, 2001.

Campbell, Joseph. *The Hero With A Thousand Faces.* Princeton, N. J.: Princeton University Press, 1968.

_____. *The Power Of The Myth.* New York: Doubleday, 1988.

Cannon, Walter B. *The Wisdom Of The Body.* New York: W. W. Norton & Company, 1963.

Capra, Fritjof. *The Tao Of Physics.* New York: Bantam, 1977.

Carson, Rachel. *Silent Spring.* New York: Houghton Mifflin, 1962.

Chodron, Pema. *Start Where You Are: A Guide To Compassionate Living.* Boston: Shambhala, 2001.

Chopra, Deepak. *Creating Health.* Boston: Houghton Mifflin Company, 1987.

_____. *Perfect Health: The Complete Mind Body Guide.* New York: Three Rivers Press, 1991.

_____. *The Way Of The Wizard: Twenty Spiritual Lessons For Creating The Life You Want.* New York: Harmony Books, 1995.

Cousins, Norman. *Anatomy Of An Illness As Perceived By The Patient.* New York: W.W. Norton & Company, 1979.

Csikszentmihalyi, Mihaly. *Creativity: The Psychology Of Discovery & Invention.* New York: Harper Collins, 1996.

Dossey, Larry. *Space, Time & Medicine.* Boston: New Science Library, Shambhala Publications, 1982.

Estes, Clarissa Pinkola. *Seeing In The Dark: Myths and Stories To Reclaim The Buried Knowing Woman.* Boulder: Sounds True, 2010.

_____. *Women Who Run With The Wolves: Myths And Stories Of The Wild Woman Archetype.* Ballantine, 1992.

Edwards, Betty. *Drawing On The Right Side Of The Brain.* Los Angeles: J.P. Tarcher, 1989.

Fanning, Patrick. *Visualization For Change: Using The Creative Power Of Your Imagination For Self-Improvement, Therapy, Healing & Pleasure.* Oakland: New Harbinger Publications, 1994.

Fields, Taylor, Weyler & Ingrasci. *Chop Wood, Carry Water: A Guide To Finding Spiritual Fulfillment In Everyday Life.* Los Angeles: J. P. Tarcher, 1984.

Feldman, David B. & Lasher, Andrew, Jr. *The End-of-Life Handbook: A Compassionate Guide To Connecting And Caring For A Dying Loved One.* Oakland: New Harbinger Publications, 2008.

Florida, Richard. *The Rise Of The Creative Class.* New York: Basic Books, 2002.

Follett, Mary Parker. *Creative Experience.* New York: Longman, Green & Co., 1924.

Gardner, Howard. *Frames Of Mind: Theory Of Multiple Intelligences.* New York: Basic Books, 1983.

Gibran, Kahlil. *The Prophet.* New York: Alfred A. Knopf, 1926.

Gawain, Shakti. *Creative Visualization.* Mill Valley, Ca.: Whatever Publishing, 1978.

Hanh, Thich Nhat. *The Miracle Of Mindfulness.* Boston: Beacon Press, 1987.

Hay, Louise L. *You Can Heal Your Life.* Santa Monica, Ca.: Hay House, 1982.

Hawking, Stephen. *The Illustrated A Brief History Of Time.* New York: Bantam, 1996.

Henri, Robert. *The Art Spirit.* New York: J. B. Lippincott, 1923.

Kelley, Tom & David. *Creative Confidence: Unleashing The Creative Potential Within Us All.* New York: Crown, 2013.

Jung, Carl Gustav. *Dreams.* Princeton, N.J.: Princeton University Press, 1974.

_____. *Man And His Symbols.* New York, Doubleday, 1964.

Kabat-Zinn, Jon. *Wherever You Go There You Are: Mindfulness Meditation In Everyday Life.* New York: Hyperion Books, 1994.

Levitin, Daniel. *This Is Your Brain On Music.* New York: Dutton, 2006.

_____. *The Organized Mind: Thinking Straight In The Age Of Information Overload.* New York: Dutton, 2014.

London, Peter. *No More Secondhand Art: Awakening The Artist Within.* Boston: Shambhala, 1989.

Maisel, Eric. *Creativity For Life.* Novato, Ca: New World Library, 2007.

McNiff, Shaun. *Art Heals: How Creativity Cures The Soul.* Boston, Shambhala, 2004.

Moore, Thomas. *Care Of The Soul.* New York: Harper Collins, 1992.

Murdock, Maureen. *Spinning Inward.* Boston: Shambhala, 1987.

Myss, Caroline. *Anatomy Of The Spirit: The Seven Stages Of Healing.* New York: Three Rivers Press, 1996.

Nicolaides, Kimon. *The Natural Way To Draw.* Boston: Houghton Mifflin & Co., 1941.

Peale, Norman Vincent. *The Power Of Positive Thinking.* New York: Prentice Hall, 1952.

Pert, Candance. *The Molecules Of Emotion: The Science Behind Mind Body Medicine.* New York: Scribner, 1997.

Robinson, Kenneth. *Out Of Our Minds; Learning To Be Creative.* New York: John Wiley & Sons, 2011.

Sacks, Oliver W. *An Anthropologist On Mars: 7 Paradoxical Tales.* New York: Vintage Books, 1995.

____. *Musicophilia: Tales Of Music And The Brain.* New York: Vintage Books, 2007.

Samuels, Michael and Lane, Mary Rockwood. *Creative Healing: How To Heal Yourself By Tapping Your Hidden Creativity.* New York: Harper Collins, 1998.

Seligman, Martin. *Authentic Happiness: Using Positive Psychology To Realize Your Potential For Lasting Fulfillment.* New York: Free Press, 2002.

Siegel, Bernie S. *Love, Medicine And Miracles.* New York: Harper Collins, 1991

Smith, Huston. *The World's Religions.* New York: Harper Collins, 1948.

Steiner, Rudolf, *Colour: Twelve Lectures by Rudolf Steiner.* East Sussex, England: Rudolf Steiner Press, 1992.

Taylor, Jill Bolte. *My Stroke Of Insight: A Brain Scientist's Personal Journey.* New York: Viking, 2008.

Van Der Kolk, Bessel. *The Body Keeps The Score: Brain, Mind, and Body in the Healing of Trauma,* New York: Penquin Books, 2014.

Weil, Andrew. *Spontaneous Healing.* New York: Ballantine Books, 1995.

Zukav, Gary. *Seat Of The Soul.* New York: Free Press, 1989.

23: Research & Resources

Learn more about the art, science, psychology, and philosophy of creative wellness. Along with my curiosity, these resources informed this work and are interesting places to begin exploring the topic. Seekers will find more university-based programs, academic publications, blogs, and online resources.

American Art Therapy Association
Resources, education, training, and events for art therapists.
www.arttherapy.org

American Dance Therapy Association
Education, training, and research in dance/movement therapy.
www.adta.org

American Healing Arts Foundation
Art therapy and wellness resources for veterans.
www.americanhealingartsfoundation.org

American Music Therapy Association
Music therapy education resources, research, and advocacy.
www.musictherapy.org

Americans for the Arts
Support for organizations and individuals who cultivate the arts.
www.americansforthearts.org

Annenberg Learner
Education resources for arts, health, science, and humanities.
www.learner.org

Laura Jaquays

ART HOPE
Creative wellness education, articles, and resources.
www.arthope.org

Brain and Creativity Institute, Dr. Antonio Damasio
University of Southern California - College of Letters, Arts & Sciences
Brain and creativity research, publications, and education.
www.dornsife.usc.edu/bci

C. Everett Koop Institute
Dartmouth College Geisel School of Medicine
Healing and the Arts Program
www.geiselmed.dartmouth.edu/koop/programs/healing

Center for Brain and Cognition, Dr. Vilayanur S. Ramachandran
University of California San Diego
Brain science and research related to the humanities.
www.cbc.ucsd.edu

Creative Education Foundation
Education resources for creative problem solving and enrichment.
www.creativeeducationfoundation.org

Dr. Jill Bolte Taylor
Information and books about the brain's resilience and creativity.
www.drjilltaylor.com

Greater Good Science Center
University of California, Berkeley
Health and wellness education, articles, and resources.
www.greatergood.berkeley.edu

Institute for Music and Neurological Function
www.musictherapy.imnf.org

International Expressive Arts Therapy Association
Education and resources in the field of expressive arts therapy.
www.ieata.org

John Hopkins School of Medicine
Education and research in the arts and medicine.
www.hopkinsmedicine.org/meart

Lesley University
Education, training, and research in the therapeutic arts,
wellness, and public health.
www.lesley.edu/academics/expressive-therapies

Library of Congress
Arts, health and wellness articles, videos, and books.
www.loc.gov

National Association for Poetry Therapy
www.poetrytherapy.org

National Coalition of Creative Arts Therapies Associations
Resources for art, dance, drama, music, and poetry therapies.
www.nccata.org

National Institute for Health
Wellness tool kit resources and articles.
www.nih.gov/health-information/your-healthiest-self-wellness-toolkits

Laura Jaquays

National Library of Medicine
Health and wellness information and research.
www.nlm.nih.gov

National Organization for Arts in Health
Initiatives and research in the arts as an integral component in
medical treatment and education, prevention, and public health.
www.thenoah.net

National Wellness Institute
Professional development and engagement opportunities
for individuals from a variety of wellness disciplines.
www.nationalwellness.org

Norman Cousins Center for Psychoneuroimmunology
Semel Institute for Neuroscience and Human Behavior
University of California Los Angeles
www.semel.ucla.edu/cousins

Omega Institute
Wellness education, enrichment, and community forums.
www.eomega.org

Psychology Today
Blogs about creative learning and behavior, and the arts in health.
www.psychologytoday.com/blog/arts-and-health

TED
TEDMed
Talks from innovators on health, wellness, science, and creativity.
www.ted.com   wwwtedmed.com

Tennenbaum Center for the Biology of Creativity
Semel Institute for Neuroscience and Human Behavior
University of California Los Angeles
www.semel.ucla.edu/creativity

The Chopra Center
Wellness resources, articles, and enrichment programs.
www.chopra.com

The Creativity Post
Resources and articles about the science of creativity in the arts,
education, psychology, business, technology, and popular culture.
www.creativitypost.com

The Foundation for Art and Healing
Initiatives to promote creative expression as an approach to
improve public health for individuals and communities.
www.artandhealing.org

The Happiness Project
Podcast by Yale professor Dr Laurie Santos
Scientific research and stories about the psychology of happiness.
www.happinesslab.fm

24: Moving Forward

ART HOPE The Way To Creative Wellness is a practical guide for healthful, artful living that explores the healing opportunities of art-making, art-taking, and art-giving. For individuals and communities, it's a common sense approach that helps people recognize and practice creativity for self-expression and self-care. Creativity is an essential life skill and our most renewable and valuable natural resource. It is the way to wellness, and the way forward, as we co-create a better world. The nonprofit ART HOPE is a resource for creative wellness education, information, and articles. Learn more at **arthope.org**.

Laura Jaquays is an educator and the founder of ART HOPE, a nonprofit dedicated to creative wellness. She teaches complementary arts-based therapies through drawing, watercolors, journal making, and origami. She established the imprint ART HOPE PRESS to publish books and curriculums about creative wellness and donates her author's proceeds to the nonprofit. Laura is a writer and artist living in Maine. Learn more about the author at **laurajaquays.com**.

www.ingramcontent.com/pod-product-compliance
Lightning Source LLC
Chambersburg PA
CBHW051444050726
47593CB00005B/1928